TONY ROMO

BEN ROETHLISBERGER

RICHARD J. BRENNER

EAST END PUBLISHING, LTD.
Miller Place, New York

AUTHOR'S NOTE: Tony Romo and Ben Roethlisberger are gifted athletes, but they both had to work hard and overcome many obstacles before they were able to achieve their dreams. And, even now, they keep working on their games, trying to become the best players that they can be.

"At each level, I've had to figure out what I had to do be successful," said Tony Romo, referring to all the work he had to do to achieve that success. "It takes me a little time, but I get there."

You can achieve your dreams, too, if you believe in yourself and work as hard to achieve your goals as Romo and Roethlisberger work to achieve theirs. And there are lots of areas for you to consider besides athletics. You might want to become an artist or a musician or a writer; or you might decide to work for world peace or to help clean the environment. The real lesson to be learned is that you can accomplish whatever you put your mind to, as long you're willing to work hard to achieve it.

This book is dedicated, as all my books are, to the children of the world. I wish that all of you could live in peaceful, loving surroundings, free from fear and bigotry of every type, and that each of you will always stride toward your sweetest dreams.

savedarfur.org

I also want to express great appreciation to everybody whose time and talents have contributed to this book, including John Douglas, Alfred Mercado, John Backus, Bob Christopher, Jamie Calsyn, Ellen Raimondo Shupp, Rob Tringali and Rich Moser, Sports Information Director Eastern Illinois University.

I also want to express sincere thanks to Ed Masessa and Janet Speakman for their continued support.

Copy Editor: John Douglas   Book Design: Alfred Mercado

Photo Credits: SportsChrome supplied the following images, all of which were photographed by **Rob Tringali**: P. 68, 71, 76 and 79. The image on P. 66 was photographed by **Clark Brooks** and supplied by the **Eastern Illinois Sports Information Dept.** The image on P. 75 was supplied by **SN/ZUMA/ICON SMI** and photographed by **Bob Leverone.** Icon SMI supplied all of the remaining photographs, as per the following, with the photographers' names in parenthesis: The cover image of Tony Romo and the image on P. 69 and 72 (**James D. Smith**); P. 65 (**Aaron Sprecher**); P. 67 (**Kevin Reece**); P. 70 (**Karl Wright**). The cover image of Ben Roethlisberger and the image on P. 73 (**Jon Sommers**); P. 74 (**David Merrill**); P. 77 and 80 (**Aaron Josefczyk**); P. 78 (**Nick Doan**).

ISBN: 0-943403-75-8 * 978-0-943403-75-5

Published by EAST END PUBLISHING, LTD.
18 Harbor Beach Road
Miller Place, NY 11764
Printed in the United States of America by R.R. Donnelley

Richard J. Brenner, America's best-selling sportswriter, has written more than 80 exciting sports titles. For details on how to order some of them, see the back of this book.

* * *

Mr. Brenner is also available to speak at schools and other venues. For details, including fees, you may e-mail him directly at: rjbrenner1@gmail.com, or write to him c/o EEP, 18 Harbor Beach Road, Miller Place, NY 11764.

AUTHOR'S MESSAGE: For many years, Native American groups have been appealing to sports teams not to use names and logos that many Native American people find offensive, such as "Redskins." Out of respect for, and in support of those appeals, I have chosen not to use such names in this book. I urge all readers who agree with this position to write to the owner of the Washington franchise, Dan Snyder, and to Roger Goodell, the commissioner of the NFL, and add your voice to those who are protesting the use of those names and logos.

TABLE OF CONTENTS

TONY ROMO

BEN ROETHLISBERGER

1   THE PLAYMAKER

Antonio (Tony) Ramiro Romo, was born April 21, 1980, in San Diego, California, the third of three children and the only boy for Joan and Ramiro Romo.

"I'm almost positive that if I'd had him first, I wouldn't have had any other children," said Joan, in joking about how much easier it had been to care for her two daughters, Danielle and Jossalyn, than for her extremely active son. "He wore me out."

Romo's parents, both natives of Racine, Wisconsin, were in San Diego because that's where Ramiro was stationed as a member of the US Navy. When he was discharged in 1982, however, the family moved back to Wisconsin, where they settled in Burlington, a small town nestled in the southeast corner of the state, about 20 miles west of Racine.

Ramiro Romo, a second-generation American, whose parents immigrated to the United States from Mexico, initially earned his living as a carpenter while the children were growing up, but eventually worked his way into building management, first as a foreman and then into his current position as a construction superintendent.

Joan Romo worked, too, at an assortment of different jobs, including one at the clubhouse counter at a local golf course. On many mornings, she would drive her son to the course, where he would sometimes play a few holes of golf before catching the bus to school.

"We had all the needs, but probably not all the wants,"

explained Joan.

Romo's main need while he was growing up was playing ball, whether it was golf, soccer or basketball.

"Whichever sport was in season, that was the one he played," recalled his father, who had played high school basketball and soccer. "He's just always loved sports and has always been very competitive, has always worked hard to do his best."

The one major sport that Romo didn't get involved with until he reached high school was football. Burlington didn't have a youth league, so he concentrated on basketball and soccer, the sports his father had played. Scott Hoffman, who coached teams in recreational leagues that Romo played on, recalled him more for his brains than for his physical talent.

"He was smart, smarter than most coaches," offered Hoffman, who is the assistant athletic director at Burlington High School. "I don't want to say he was lazy, but he would always look for shortcuts when it came to doing drills. Tony was all about getting to game day."

Romo started out playing soccer during the fall term of his freshman year at Burlington High School, but soon switched over to football. In his sophomore year, Romo might have wished he'd stuck with soccer, however, because he broke a finger and missed most of the football season. The finger healed in time for the hoops season, however, and Romo proceeded to impress the basketball coach, Steve Berezowitz, with his dedication as much as his talent.

Romo showed that his hunger to play was so strong that even a snowstorm couldn't stop him from getting to a game. He had waited at the house, as planned, for his father to pick him up. After a while, he realized that his dad must

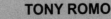

have been delayed by the weather and knew that he wasn't carrying a cell phone, so he hopped on his bike and pedaled through the snow to try to reach the school bus that was scheduled to take the basketball team to a game at East Troy High School. By the time he reached his school, however, the bus had already left. Undaunted, Romo got right back on his bike and started pedaling the snowy roads, hoping that he'd be able to make the 15 mile trek quickly enough to make it to East Troy for at least the second half of the game. Romo's father was finally able to catch up with him about halfway through the trip, and then didn't have the heart to punish him for pulling such a dangerous stunt.

"How could I ground him?" asked Romo's dad. "I was just so glad that I caught up to him and that he was OK."

"Good thing that he made it, because we needed him," said coach Berezowitz. "Tony had a fantastic game and we wound up winning the game, finally, but not until the second overtime."

Romo started to develop as a quality quarterback in his junior year, under the guidance of Steve Gerber, who was the head football coach at Burlington from 1997-2002. Unlike many, if not most of the football teams that play in the cold climes of the upper Midwest, where fields can get slick, hard and snow-covered later in the season, Gerber eschewed more conservative, straight ahead offenses, and, instead, schooled the Demons in a wide-open spread attack. The offense places a premium on a quick, athletic quarterback, one who can run as well as pass. It also calls for the quarterback to make split-second decisions based upon what he sees when he comes to the line of scrimmage. Romo would come to the line with four to five different play options, make his read, and then call the specific play from among the possibilities. In Romo, Gerber had uncovered a package of skills and smarts that was an ideal match for the scheme.

"His intelligence showed all the time, but especially after the ball was snapped," said Gerber, who currently teaches social studies at the school. "He had the uncanny ability to react on the run and make good choices, which is an unusual talent, especially at the high school level. The normal prep school quarterback that I worked with could see one side of the field, and maybe get as far as the second read, but only on that same side of the field. Tony, though, was one of those kids who could look from left to right, come back to the left side and read the secondary. It's a gift that not too many people have."

Although Romo is blessed with physical talent and a quick mind, his accomplishments also owed a great deal to his preparation and motivation.

When he wasn't playing or practicing, Romo was wearing out tapes of basketball legends like Pete Maravich, and football greats, including the now-retired Green Bay Packers' quarterback, Brett Favre. Romo also kept a pad by his side, so that he could take notes while he watched the tapes, and when he went to bed, he took the pad with him, so that if he thought of a new play or a new move while he was asleep, he could wake up and write it down before he forgot all about it.

Romo didn't merely want to get better, he took every action that he could to develop his talents and fulfill whatever potential he had.

Romo continued to improve the following year when, according to Steve Berezowitz, he made a quantum leap in his attitude between his final two years at Burlinton.

"Tony really grew up between his junior and senior year; as a person, as a student, and as an athlete," said Berezowitz, who has become a close friend of his former player.

Over the course of his final two years at Burlington, Romo produced a great many gridiron highlights while throwing 42 touchdown passes but, despite his dynamic leadership, the Demons still lost more games than they won. Romo had also excelled in basketball, and in his senior season he averaged 24.3 points, nine rebounds, and six assists per game as the Demons' high-scoring point guard, and finished as the runner-up for county player of the year to future NBA All-Star Caron Butler. But while he soared, the hoops team, like the football squad, took a nosedive, and finished with a losing record.

Although some people thought that he had more upside in basketball than he did in football, Romo decided that at 6-2, he had a higher ceiling on the gridiron than he did on the hardwood.

"Eventually, I turned to football because I felt, size-wise, that sport offered me the best chance to advance to the next level," recalled Romo. "Once I made the decision, I just went full force with it."

Despite his decision, his dedication and his individual accomplishments, Romo didn't attract attention from any of the big-time Division I-A colleges, and only one school, Eastern Illinois, a Division I-AA school, offered him a football scholarship.

"He was just one of those kids who flew under the radar a little bit," said Steve Berezowitz. "But if you watched him play, he wowed you, believe me."

Interestingly, the Panthers hadn't even scouted Romo as a football player, but one of their assistant coaches, Roy

Wittke, had received newspaper clips from his parents, who live in Racine. After he'd watched some tape of Romo on the gridiron, Wittke's interest was whetted by what he saw. Since the football season was over and done with, however, he decided to drive the four hours from Charlestown, Illinois, where EI is located, to Burlington, to see what the kid could do on a basketball court, just so he could get a live look at his athleticism and see how he handled himself.

"Every time a play needed to me made, a big bucket or a rebound, Tony was in the middle of it," recalled Wittke. "I sensed that he had something special about him."

Although Wittke liked what he had seen, he still had to do a hard sell on Bob Spoo, the head football coach, who finally relented and offered Romo a partial scholarship.

"We hadn't bothered to watch him play football, but Roy had watched him play the point for the Burlington basketball team," recalled Spoo. "He convinced me that Tony had great leadership qualities and the ability to make plays. In any sport, that's what you look for, leaders and playmakers."

2　GETTING IN LINE

When Coach Wittke recruited Romo, he didn't make any promises about playing time. In fact, Romo was told that the school already had a starting quarterback and that he would have to get in line and work hard if he wanted to eventually earn the starting role.

In 1998, his first season at EI, the coaching staff decided to red-shirt Romo, which meant that he could practice with the team, but that he couldn't play in any games. This is a strategy that allows coaches to stockpile incoming players when they're not immediately needed, and it also prevents a player from losing one of his four years of college eligibility just sitting on the bench, by allowing him to extend his college career by one year.

The decision put Romo in the unaccustomed position of being a sideline cheerleader, instead of a game-time athlete, and the situation gnawed at his confidence. At one point, he became so frustrated and discouraged that he even talked about the possibility of dropping football and seeing if he could make the basketball team.

Coach Spoo, meanwhile, had started to regret recruiting him, because Romo had been slow to adapt to the speed of the college game during practices, and he also seemed to lack the drive to turn up his accelerator. In fact, if Roy Wittke hadn't talked him out of it, Coach Spoo was all set to switch Romo to tight end the following year.

Wittke also had a verbal showdown with Romo, telling

him that he needed to pick up his pace and dedicate himself to doing the things that he needed to do to progress as a quarterback.

"I really got after Tony, laid it all out and told him what I expected from him, in no uncertain terms" said Wittke. "He took it to heart and came back and showed marked improvement during spring practice. In my mind, if there was one incident that turned him around, that was it."

The following year, Romo saw action in three games, including two fill-in starts when the senior starter, Anthony Buich, was out with an injury. But his play didn't do anything to indicate that his college career was about to take off. In between seasons, however, Romo put in countless hours watching film, refining his skills and working on his throwing mechanics.

"The first time I met him, I walked into the stadium and he was watching tape with the defensive players, because the offensive guys weren't there yet," recalled Roc Bellantoni, who was the linebackers coach at EI at the time. "Obviously, he has talent, but it's his drive and competitiveness that puts him over the top. Sometimes, I'd be driving home from work at midnight, and there was Tony, playing catch in the middle of the street with one of the freshman quarterbacks. He was relentless. I just think that he feels that there's nothing that he can't accomplish on a football field."

All the work that Romo put in throughout the spring and summer paid off big time in the fall of 2000, when he threw for 27 touchdown passes in 11 starts, led the Panthers into the Division I-AA playoffs, and was named the Ohio Valley Conference Player of the Year.

"His success didn't come about by accident," said Coach Spoo. "He was like a gym rat. He would stay after practice and work on throws he hadn't been happy with. He's not afraid to work, and all that work started to pay big dividends."

Romo raised the bar higher still in his junior season, as he completed a career-high 66.7 percent of his passes, and led all Division I-AA quarterbacks in passing efficiency with an off-the-charts 178.3 rating. His performance helped lead the Panthers to a second consecutive OVC championship, and also earned him his second straight Conference Player of the Year award, as well as a Third-Team All-America selection by the Associated Press.

"I knew that he had a great deal of ability when I saw him in high school, but I can't, honestly, say that I knew he'd develop into that good a quarterback," said Wittke. "It just goes to show what can happen when you marry hard work to talent."

Romo started his senior season with a bang against a pair of Division I-A teams, as he bagged four TD passes against Hawaii and followed that up by completing 23 of 35 passes against Big 12 power Kansas State. Unfortunately for the Panthers, those performances couldn't prevent the team from being overwhelmed by superior programs, and they lost both of those games by staggering scores. But after those two drubbings, the Panthers went on an eight-game winning streak, and Romo continued his high-octane roar by torching Tennessee Tech with four touchdown passes, and then threw for another pair of scores and 359 yards against the Colonels of Eastern Kentucky. But the play that people still talk about from the Eastern Kentucky game was made not with his right arm, but with his two feet, as he eluded a clutch of Colonels' defenders with only a few seconds left to play and scrambled into the end zone on an eight-yard TD scamper that lifted the Panthers to a 25-24 win.

The Panthers' winning streak came to a stop in the last game of the regular season, when Murray State eked out a 37-35 win. Their 8-3 record had earned them their third consecutive trip to the I-AA playoffs, but they were blown out of the stadium by Western Illinois, 48-9, as Romo ended his college career with his third straight first-round playoff loss.

Although his final game had ended with a defeat, Romo had compiled an outstanding senior season, with 34 touchdown tosses, a single-season school record 3,165 passing yards, and a 63.4 completion percentage. His 258 completions broke the conference record, and his passing skills were the main ingredient in allowing the Panthers to post a 37.7 scoring average, making them one of the highest-scoring teams in the nation.

"He improved every year, and there wasn't any magic, and it didn't happen by chance," said Wittke. "He just threw constantly. When you saw Tony, you could count on seeing a football in his hands."

His excellence was confirmed when he was named the winner of the 2002 Walter Payton Award, which is given each year to the top offensive player in Division I-AA. Romo was the first player from the OVC to win the award.

"Walter Payton exemplified what dedication and commitment can accomplish," said Coach Spoo, in speaking of the late running back, who set the NCAA record for points scored while playing for the Division I-AA Jackson State Tigers, and then went on to a Hall of Fame career with the Chicago Bears. "Tony is a classic example of what can be achieved by following Payton's qualities. Tony earned the respect of his teammates by his work ethic. No matter how much individual success he achieved, he was still one of the hardest-working players right up to his final collegiate game. That work ethic and leadership resulted in his teammates expecting to succeed. Tony is a quality young man, who led his team to victory."

Romo, who had come to Eastern Illinois with only a partial scholarship, left the campus with First-Team All-America honors, and near the top of the school's list for career passing yards and completions, while establishing a new OVC mark for career touchdown passes with 85. He had led the Panthers to three straight Division I-AA playoff games, and completely justified the faith that Roy Wittke had placed in him five years earlier.

"There are a thousand Tony Romos out there, players with high-level potential," said Wittke, who was named the Division I-AA Assistant Coach of the Year in 2002 for being the guiding force in the Panthers' offense. "But not too many of them are willing to put in the effort that it takes to develop that raw talent. He didn't have that type of drive when he came here but, by the time he left us, he was the best practice player I've ever been around. Tony didn't cheat himself or the program. He worked long and hard to turn his potential into performance."

3   THE DALLAS DOLDRUMS

Although Romo had been the sparkplug in the Panthers' offense and done everything that he could do to fulfill every ounce of potential that he possessed, NFL scouts questioned his overall ability and the fact that he had played in a system designed to show him off at his best.

"For starters, a lot of people questioned his arm strength," said Russell Lande, a former NFL talent scout who now runs an independent scouting service. "He didn't show a great arm by NFL standards, and he played in an offense that was designed to highlight the quarterback. A lot of teams thought that he might just be a product of the system, rather than a legitimate pro prospect."

Romo's chance to be drafted was also hurt by his poor performance at the NFL Combine, an invitation only pre-draft workout for prospects hoping to impress NFL teams.

"I felt good, like it was a step for me to show people what I could do, but I didn't throw as well as I wanted to," admitted Romo, who was part of a quarterback mix that also included Carson Palmer, Byron Leftwich and Kyle Boller, all of whom would be picked in the first round of the draft. "I'm pretty realistic about my talents, and I felt that I wasn't as good as some of the other guys there. In my heart of hearts I knew those guys were better than me. I really struggled that day, and the fact of the matter is that I just wasn't ready at that time."

In the end, there were so many doubts that when the NFL

conducted its 2003 draft, all 32 teams passed on Romo.

"We had reports on him, because he was very productive in college," said Mark Dominik, the director of pro personnel for the Tampa Bay Buccaneers, a team that under head coach Jon Gruden tends to stockpile quarterbacks as though they are about to become extinct. "But his mechanics were a little scary. He didn't have a great release, which is an absolute essential for an NFL quarterback. He was on our radar screen but, like everyone else, we took him off our board before the draft."

Although none of the league's teams had wanted to spend a draft pick on him, Romo did get a few free agent offers, but not from either of the teams that he had hoped to hear from; the Green Bay Packers, who he had rooted for while growing up, and the Chicago Bears, who he had followed while playing at EI. One of the teams that did make an offer was the Denver Broncos, whose head coach, Mike Shanahan, had been a quarterback at Eastern Illinois in the 1970s, and later an assistant coach for the Panthers.

Romo, however, decided to accept an offer from the Dallas Cowboys, whose interest in Romo was initiated by another former Panthers' quarterback, Sean Payton, who at the time was an assistant head coach and quarterbacks coach for the Cowboys. In fact, Payton, who had graduated from EI in 1986, was the quarterback, who had held the career TD passing mark that Romo had eclipsed.

Payton was part of a new coaching regime that had been brought in by the recently-hired head coach, Bill Parcells. The gruff, sarcastic and demanding Parcells, a Hall of Fame coach who had earlier presided over the resurrection of three fumbling franchises—the New York Giants, with whom he had won a pair of Super Bowls, the New England Patriots, who he had coached to an AFC Championship, and the New York Jets, who he had restored to respectability—had been hired by the Dallas owner and general manager, Jerry Jones, to restore luster to the tarnished star of a franchise, whose fabled history had been followed by a stumble into mediocrity.

The Cowboys, whose past glories and national popularity had earned them the title of America's Team, had, for a long time, been one of the NFL's elite franchises. They were a dominant team in the 1970s, when they won their first two Super Bowl titles, and they reclaimed their mantle of greatness in the 1990s when they won a trio of Super Bowls between 1993 and 1996, to become the first team to win three Super Bowls in four years. Only two other franchises, the Pittsburgh Steelers and the San Francisco 49ers, have been able to match the Cowboys' total of five Super Bowl championships, but Dallas stands alone as the only franchise to appear in eight Super Bowls.

The Cowboys' past success hadn't been limited to their eight NFC championships. They had played with such a high level of proficiency for so long that they set a league record by posting a winning season for 20 consecutive years from 1965 to 1985. Then, after a few faltering years, they had been revitalized by an influx of future Hall of Famers, including Emmitt Smith, Michael Irvin, and Troy Aikman, and they returned to their winning ways for the first half of the 1990s, when they were the dominant team in the NFL.

But the greatness that Dallas' fans had come to expect from their team started to fade away, like aging memories, as the Cowboys' losing seasons started to multiply, with three consecutive 5-11 seasons from 2000-2002. And their last playoff win, which had occurred in 1996, kept slipping farther into the receding past.

The great Dallas teams had been blessed with a string of outstanding quarterbacks, including a pair of Hall of Famers, Roger Staubach and Troy Aikman. Staubach, who was a feared scrambler as well as a superior passer, earned six Pro Bowl selections in his nine seasons as a starter, from 1971-1979, and led the Cowboys to four NFC Championships and the franchise's first two Super Bowl titles. Aikman, the first overall pick in the 1989 draft, piloted the Cowboys to 90 wins in the 1990s, the most victories ever posted by a quarterback in a single decade. He also led the Cowboys to their final three Super Bowl titles and was selected to play in six Pro Bowls, before retiring after the end of the 2000 season.

When the Cowboys assembled for the start of training camp, Parcells didn't have any illusions about the quarterbacks that came to compete for roster spots in 2003. As hard as he looked, he didn't see anyone who even remotely reminded him of Staubach or Aikman. Besides Romo, who Parcells certainly wasn't counting on to do any heavy lifting, the cast that reported to camp consisted of a trio of young and, by NFL standards, relatively undistinguished signal-callers, Quincy Carter, Chad Hutchinson and Clint Stoerner.

Carter, a first round pick in the 2001 draft, had become the starting quarterback as a rookie, more by default than design, and his performance had been decidedly uneven. He'd continued as the starter for the first seven games of the 2002 season, when he had a blow-up with Jerry Jones, and was replaced by Hutchinson for the remainder of the season. Carter, however, was Parcells' pick to lead the Cowboys into the 2003 season, while Hutchinson, who had had a very brief and very ineffective career as a major league pitcher prior to signing with Dallas, wound up as Carter's backup. Romo, meanwhile, was named the third string quarterback, just barely beating out Stoerner, who had been with the Cowboys since 2000. After being dropped by Dallas, Stoerner was signed by the Miami Dolphins for one season, but he never made it into a game, and then his NFL career came to a quiet end.

The fact of the matter is that if the Cowboys had had a stronger cast of quarterbacks, Romo probably wouldn't have been able to make the roster and been given the time and opportunity to show that he could, in due course, become a playmaker in the NFL. To this day, Romo isn't even sure just why Parcells decided to keep him instead of Stoerner.

"I think Bill saw some of the instinctive things that I did on the field during practices, but I don't really know," said Romo. "I guess he thought that I could, eventually, be pretty good, and that's why he kept me around."

4 HANGING IN AND HANGING ON

While Romo had made the team, his entire output for the 2003 season occurred in the preseason, when he threw for 137 yards, completing nine passes in 17 attempts, and connecting for one touchdown and one interception. After that, when Sunday came around, Romo was nailed to the bench. Although he obviously didn't have the benefit of playing behind a highly skilled, veteran quarterback, who he could watch and learn from, Romo was fortunate to have a top-notch coaching staff, which worked behind the scenes to help him develop his talent and instruct him on how to get his game up to NFL standards. Romo, meanwhile, did everything that he could to speed his development, as he displayed the same gym-rat habits that he had at Eastern Illinois.

"A lot of people in Tony's situation, coming in as an undrafted free agent, fourth on the depth chart, just kind of go through the motions, spend a few weeks in an NFL training camp, and then get on with the rest of their lives," said Sean Payton. "But Tony was used to bucking the odds. He knew what it was like to be in the back of the bus. He hadn't been recruited by a major college, and even at Eastern Illinois, he had had to work hard to win the starting job. He wasn't going to quit or have his confidence crushed by being low man on the totem pole with the Cowboys. He knew, from experience, that hard work pays off, and that's exactly how he approached his first year in Dallas. He went to work on his passing technique, and he got bleary-eyed watching tape of opposing defenses, learning what it takes to be an NFL quarterback."

Carter, meanwhile, wound up doing a decent job during the 2003 season, and the Cowboys, behind the league's top-rated defense, posted a surprising 10-6 mark, before they went one and out in the postseason.

Carter had definitely shown some promise, but the 21 interceptions that he had thrown also showed that he was still very much a work in progress. Parcells addressed those concerns early in the team's preparations for the 2004 season.

"The interceptions are my biggest concern, said Parcells, who has an extremely low tolerance for quarterbacks who can't protect the football. "And I can't tell you how he is going to respond to pressure situations this year until I see him perform in them."

Since there isn't anything that can draw the wrath of Parcells more than turnovers, the coach decided to bring in some quarterback reinforcements for the 2004 season, and he chose someone old and someone new to wear the Dallas blue.

The someone old was Vinny Testaverde, a well-traveled, strong-armed 17-year veteran, who had played for Parcells when both of them were with the Jets. Parcells liked having a veteran quarterback on hand, a player who could learn the offense quickly, read defenses, and be ready to step in and provide instant leadership and steady play in case Carter, the presumed starter, was ineffective or went down with an injury.

The someone new was Drew Henson, who had been a high school All-American and considered by many to be the next great college quarterback when he went to the University of Michigan. The Wolverines' coaching staff couldn't wait to get Henson on the field, and he challenged Tom Brady, an upper classman, for the starting role during the 1998 and 1999 seasons. But it wasn't until 2000, after Brady had graduated and been drafted by the New England Patriots, that Henson finally took full control of the starting job. Henson went on to throw 18 TD passes in his junior season, but then he decided to sidetrack his very promising football career, forego his senior season, and concentrate his efforts on professional baseball.

"When you look at the last three games he played at Michigan, you'd swear he'd be the No. 1 overall pick in the NFL draft," raved Gil Brandt, an NFL.com analyst, who had been the main front office architect of the Cowboys teams from the 1960s through the 1980s. "He's got everything you need: arm strength, mobility, and he's bright."

The idea that Henson might also make it in the big leagues wasn't at all far-fetched. He had been an extraordinary high school baseball player, who had hit 70 career home runs, which was a prep school record, and been selected as the 1998 USA Today High School Baseball Player of the Year. The New York Yankees had spent a third round draft pick on Henson, despite knowing that he intended to enroll at Michigan and play football. Unfortunately for Henson and the Yankees, who had invested a great deal of money in him, Henson struggled to work his way up to the majors and quit the game in 2004, after compiling a total of nine big league base hits.

Despite the fact that Henson hadn't played a down at any level in three years, Jerry Jones was so intrigued with Henson's potential to be a top-flight quarterback that he traded a third round draft pick to the Houston Texans to obtain his rights. That move could rightly be seen as a lack of faith in Romo's ability to ever develop into the team's starting signal-caller.

In fact, with training camp just over the horizon, there didn't seem to be any room on the Cowboys' roster for Romo, who ranked fifth on the team's depth chart. Hutchinson, however, was cut in July, although he was quickly signed by the Chicago Bears to back up Rex Grossman. After one season in that role, Hutchinson was dropped the following summer, which brought his brief and ineffective NFL career to a dead end.

But, that still left Romo as the team's fourth quarterback, which meant that it didn't seem likely that he would be on the roster when the season started. On August 4th, however, less than a week into camp, Quincy Carter was suddenly released, with Parcells stating that the quarterback could not be trusted to lead the team. According to the Cowboys, a failed drug test was the major factor, but not the only one. Carter was quickly signed as a backup by the Jets, and helped them reach the playoffs, but after one season in New York, he was unable to hook up with any NFL team. Since then, Carter has twice been arrested for marijuana possession, but he is currently attempting to straighten out his life and to resurrect his once-promising career with the Kansas City Brigade of the Arena Football League.

5 A MINDSET FOR GREATNESS

Instead of getting handed a one-way ticket out of Dallas, as had seemed likely only a few weeks earlier, Romo suddenly found himself in a spirited competition with Henson to be Testaverde's backup. Given the opportunity and playing time that he probably would not have received if Carter was still with the team, Romo went on to impress the Cowboys' coaching staff during the preseason by connecting on 24 of 39 pass attempts for 273 yards, one TD and a pair of interceptions. That showing convinced Parcells to name Romo as the backup signal-caller at the start of the 2004 season, but he and Henson continued to jockey for the spot and, by the end of the season, Romo had slipped a notch and was the team's third-string quarterback.

Although Testaverde had had an up-and-down year on the field, and the Cowboys slipped back to a 6-10 record, Romo had benefited from watching how the veteran went about his job, and from listening to the tips that Testaverde passed along during practices and film sessions.

"I knew that I still had a lot to learn, and seeing the way Vinny handled himself and ran the team was like getting an advanced degree in quarterbacking," said Romo. "It also helped, psychologically, that I got to be the team's holder, which allowed me to feel that I was at least making a contribution, instead of just sitting on the bench the way I had in 2003."

Eddie George, who had been a four-time Pro Bowl

running back for the Tennessee Titans before signing with Dallas in 2004, had taken notice of how intently Romo studied Testaverde, learning what worked as well as what didn't work, and figuring out how he could apply the lessons to his own talents.

"Tony was like a sponge," said George, whose nine-year NFL career came to a close after that single season with Dallas. "He soaked up all the knowledge that Vinny had. Now, he's utilizing what Vinny taught him, but he's doing it with his own style. I think he was figuring out what it took to be great. He wasn't going to settle on being a backup. He has the mindset for greatness."

Parcells had appreciated Testaverde's contributions, but instead of re-signing him for the 2005 season, he decided to try to upgrade the position by bringing in another veteran, Drew Bledsoe. It was another quarterback reunion for Parcells, who had taken Bledsoe with the No. 1 overall pick in the 1993 draft, when he had been the Patriots' head coach. Three years later, Bledsoe, who was a three-time Pro Bowler during his nine seasons in New England, led the Patriots to an appearance in Super Bowl XXXI, where they were beaten by the Brett Favre-led Green Bay Packers, 35-21. Bledsoe had remained as the Patriots' starter until early in the 2001 season, when he suffered an injury that opened the door for his backup, Tom Brady. By the time Bledsoe had recovered, Bill Belichick, who had become the team's head coach, decided to stay with Brady, a second-year player, who was younger and more mobile than Bledsoe. Brady had quickly validated Belichick's decision by piloting the Patriots into the playoffs and on to the first of their three Super Bowl wins with him at the helm, 20-17 over the St. Louis Rams. Bledsoe, who had taken issue with losing his starting job over an injury, was traded to the Buffalo Bills before the start of the 2002 season. He went on to post big numbers that first year with the Bills, including 4,359 passing yards and 24 touchdown passes, while earning his fourth Pro Bowl selection. But he was let go after the end of the 2004 season, when the Bills decided to go with a younger quarterback, J.P. Losman.

With the 33-year-old Bledsoe designated as the starter for the 2005 season, Romo and Henson continued their duel for the backup job, but Romo, with another solid training camp and superior preseason performances, came out on top.

"The kid hung in there," said Parcells. "Some of the guys that come into the league get discouraged when they don't have instant success, and it shows in their attitude and performance. Those types usually don't stay around very long. But Romo took advantage of the opportunities that we gave him, and didn't brood about what he couldn't control."

Bledsoe, who started all 16 regular season games, led the Cowboys on five game-winning drives in the fourth quarter or overtime. Those wins helped to keep Dallas in the playoff race until the final week of the season, and while it was disappointing that they fell short of making it into the postseason, their 9-7 record was certainly a step up from the losing record that the team had posted the year before.

The strong-armed Bledsoe had shown that he still had plenty of mileage left in his right arm by throwing for 23 touchdown passes and 3,639 yards, marking the ninth time that he had gone over the 3,000-yard mark. On the downside, though, he had turned the ball over 25 times, including 17 picks and eight lost fumbles, and his lack of mobility had been a major factor in the 49 sacks that he had suffered.

Romo, meanwhile, had completed his third season in the NFL, and had yet to throw his first pass. Except for being the holder on field goals and point-after attempts, his time on the field during that span, consisted of taking a knee to run out the clock on the final drive of an October game against the Philadelphia Eagles. Romo never complained about being No. 2 behind Bledsoe, but he was frustrated by the fact that he didn't even get to play in the season finale, although the Cowboys knew that they had been eliminated from postseason play an hour before the start of their game.

"I never questioned the coaching staff about their decision to make Drew the starter, and to keep riding him as long as we had a chance to reach the playoffs," said Romo. "I mean, his record speaks for itself. But, I certainly would have liked to get a chance to play in that last game. I'm a competitor, and at some point, just practicing and not playing gets old. I wanted to be able to go out on the field and test myself and, hopefully, to show the staff and my teammates that I could deliver the goods."

6   TEN LITTLE WORDS

With Bledsoe set to return for a second season in Dallas, Romo's prospects for playing time didn't appear to be any brighter in 2006 than they had been in his previous three seasons. But he did retain and even solidify his position on the Dallas depth chart, while the team decided to sever their ties to Drew Henson. The failure of the former wunderkind to successfully launch his NFL career became another textbook example of the fact that potential and pedigree do not guarantee performance.

While Henson tried, unsuccessfully, to secure a backup spot with the Minnesota Vikings, Romo went on to excel in the Cowboys preseason games, completing just under 70 percent of his passes. In the fourth and last of the preseason contests, Romo raised his productivity to ridiculous heights when he threw for 349 yards against the San Francisco 49ers in just a shade over a half a game. Although Bledsoe was still the undisputed starting quarterback, Romo's progress did not go unnoticed by Parcells.

"He showed me some things that I hadn't seen from him before then," said Parcells, who usually doles out compliments the way a miser hands out thousand dollar bills. "He played with more control, ran the plays the way they were designed, and showed that he had the ability to run through his progressions and find the open receiver."

Based on what they had seen of how Romo handled himself in the preseason games, the Cowboys decided to extend his contract through the 2007 season. It wasn't a huge commitment and the dollars, by NFL standards, weren't substantial, even for a backup quarterback. The deal was like a pat on the back, rather than an embrace, which told Romo that the Cowboys liked him, but they weren't sure that they loved him.

The evident progress that he had made, however, prompted some people in Dallas to start whispering that maybe it was time to turn the Cowboys' reins over to the younger, more mobile Romo. When the season started, though, it was Bledsoe who led the Cowboys onto the field against the Jaguars in Jacksonville. Bledsoe, however, didn't do anything to increase his job security, as he suffered two sacks and threw three interceptions, two of which set up Jacksonville touchdowns in the Cowboys' 24-17 loss.

"Too many mistakes," said a tight-lipped Parcells. "We had our chances. We just couldn't get it all together today. It's disappointing. It really is."

Suddenly, the whispers of a looming quarterback controversy started to grow louder, and Bledsoe's response to those murmurings grew testy.

"I don't think about any of it," said Bledsoe, although his words were hard to accept at face value, given his history of having been replaced by younger, more mobile quarterbacks in Boston and Buffalo. "It doesn't bother me one bit. I just go out and play ball."

The tough loss and Bledsoe's poor performance had even overshadowed the Dallas debut of All-Pro wide receiver Terrell Owens, who collared six passes, including a sensational 21-yard touchdown catch on which he turned twice before cradling the ball into his hands. Owens had come to the Cowboys after successful but controversial stays with the 49ers and then the Eagles, during which he had ripped his quarterbacks, but he refused to bark about Bledsoe's miscues.

"It's a team effort, it's a team loss," said T.O., playing a supportive role, instead of the destructive one that he had acted out in his two previous NFL stops. "Sometimes you connect and sometimes you don't. Drew has confidence in himself and in me, and we'll just go from there."

After the team returned to Dallas, Parcells did his part to defuse the idea that he was going to make a quarterback change anytime soon by telling the media that there was no quarterback controversy as far as he was concerned, and that Bledsoe was his chosen one. He also made it clear that he wasn't going to allow the media or the Dallas fans to influence, let alone dictate who he played.

"I know you folks would be happy to turn this news conference into a *blame-day* session," said Parcells, with obvious sarcasm, as he addressed the media. "I know that Drew could have played better, and I'm hopeful that he will. But I am going to give him an opportunity to do that.

"I told you that I was getting Romo ready to play," added Parcells. "And at some point in time, I'm hopeful that I will be able to play him this year. Now, I don't know when, where, or under what circumstances. But that shouldn't be the story of the day, because it's a non-story."

Bledsoe did seem to steady the ship, as the Cowboys bounced back in their next two games, a 27-10 win at home against Washington, their arch-rivals, and a 45-14 road triumph against the Tennessee Titans. It was the first start for the Titans' rookie quarterback, Vince Young, and the Cowboys' defense completely hogtied the former University of Texas star, as they picked off two of his passes and forced him into a pair of fumbles.

The Cowboys' next game, in Philadelphia, was hyped beyond all reason by the media because it marked the return of Terrell Owens to the City of Brotherly Love. It was his first game against the Eagles since he had sandbagged their quarterback and his former teammate, Donovan McNabb, following the team's loss in Super Bowl XXXIX. The following year, 2005, T.O continued to feud with the team, which eventually resulted in his being suspended by the Eagles for four games—starting with Philadelphia's eighth game—and then deactivated by them for the remainder of the season. But T.O. had only had 3 catches for 45 yards in his much-ballyhooed return to Philadelphia, as the Eagles rallied in the second half to drub Dallas, 38-24, and some fingers started to point at Bledsoe, who suffered three picks and seven sacks.

On one of Bledsoe's interceptions, Owens had been wide open deep in Eagles' territory, but the pass was so under-thrown that T.O. didn't even get a chance to make a play on the ball. Owens immediately showed his displeasure by raising his arms in futility.

"It's frustrating," said T.O., who also made it clear that he was unhappy with the scant number of passes that were directed at him. "Opportunities were there and we didn't take advantage of them."

Owens wasn't alone in feeling that the Cowboys weren't operating at full capacity when he wasn't a centerpiece of the team's offense.

"I was surprised Terrell didn't have more catches; that was not our plan," said Jerry Jones, which was either a veiled criticism of Bledsoe, the play calling, or both.

When it comes to sacks, the offensive line is usually the

chief culprit. The fact that Bledsoe didn't have the speed or quickness to elude defenders, however, was a definite liability. Even more troubling, perhaps, was the fact that after all his years in the league, he didn't have the wherewithal to avoid at least some of those seven sacks by simply throwing the ball away.

The offense continued to sputter the following week during the first half of their game against the lowly Houston Texans, but then it suddenly sprang to life and piled up 31 second-half points, and the Cowboys rolled to a 34-6 win in front of their hometown fans.

Although he threw for only 178 yards, Bledsoe had played a decent game, which included a pair of touchdown passes to Owens, who hadn't made it into the end zone in his previous three games, his longest scoring drought since the 2000 season.

Those touchdowns had seemed to defuse the friction that had been developing between Bledsoe and Owens, who still felt that he wasn't being thrown to nearly enough.

"I told him, 'Dude, just trust me,'" said Owens, referring to what he had said to Bledsoe. "I know how to play the game. When the ball is in the air, I know how to go get it."

It also pleased Cowboys' owner Jerry Jones, the man who had shelled out the dollars to bring the gifted and volatile receiver to Dallas.

"It was T.O.'s day," said Jones. "I'm glad that we signed him."

For the most part, the team's reaction to the win, which gave the Cowboys a 3-2 record, seemed subdued, as though the victory had merely served as a release from the tension that had been building around Bledsoe and the offense.

"Bledsoe was efficient, he managed the game well," said

Parcells, while also suggesting that there was still a certain spark missing from the offense. "But sometimes you have to rely on your quarterback to carry the load. I just hope he can play with more consistency."

Almost lost in the collective sigh of relief had been the late-game insertion of Romo, who completed his first two NFL passes, a 33-yard toss to wide receiver Sam Hurd, and then a two-yard floater to Owens that had closed out the scoring.

"I can't tell you how thrilled I am to finally get the chance to throw a pass in a regular season game," said Romo, who was a perfect 2-for-2. "I just hope I don't have to wait another four years to throw my next pass."

It's certainly isn't unusual for a backup quarterback to be given a few snaps at mop-up time. In fact, if anything was unusual about this instance it was that it had taken four years for it to happen. The occurrence seemed so mundane and ordinary that Parcells devoted just one sentence to the subject in his weekly news conference.

"Glad to get Romo in there for a little bit," said Parcells, as he opened and closed the subject with ten little words.

7　SOME GOOD, SOME BAD

The following week the Cowboys were hosts to the Giants, one of their divisional rivals in the National Football Conference East, who had traveled to Texas Stadium for a nationally-televised Monday Night game.

The Dallas offense, which had seemed to straighten itself out the previous week, had once against turned stagnant, and the team went into the locker room at halftime trailing by a 12-7 score. It had been another tough start for Bledsoe, who was picked off twice and sacked four times, including once for a safety when he was tackled in the Dallas end zone. His second interception, at the Giants' 1-yard line with less than two minutes left in the half, prevented the Cowboys from wresting the lead away from the Giants and going into the locker room with some momentum.

"That was a bad one," said Parcells. "The ball should have gone to the other side. That's where the play was designed to go."

At some point between that interception, which would turn out to be the last NFL pass thrown by Bledsoe, and the end of the halftime intermission, Parcells decided that the offense wasn't performing at the level that he thought that it should be, and that a change in quarterbacks might help to kick-start the engine. Before the Cowboys filed out of the locker room for the second half, an assistant coach passed along the message to Romo that he would be starting the second half.

As soon as the fans in Texas Stadium saw Romo run onto the field, they let out a huge roar of approval. If anyone thought that Romo would ride to the rescue and pull out the game for the Cowboys, however, their hopes were quickly dented when his first pass was tipped by Giants' defensive end Michael Strahan and picked off by linebacker Antonio Pierce. Three plays later, Giants' quarterback Eli Manning connected on a 13-yard touchdown pass to tight end Jeremy Shockey, which stretched their lead to 19-7.

That first pick was the start of a Dr. Jekyll and Mr. Hyde performance by Romo, who went on to toss another pair of interceptions, as well as a couple of touchdown passes and a 2-point conversion, while completing 14-of-25 passes for 227 yards.

Parcells didn't make any attempt to hide his displeasure with the sloppy play that had resulted in another Dallas defeat, 36-22, which dropped their record to 3-3.

"That was a really poor performance," said Parcells. "The same recipe for disaster that we've been cooking up since the opening game. Turnovers. Big plays early in the game. They outplayed us. They out-coached us. They out-everythinged us. I'm ashamed to put a team out there that played like that."

But his reaction to Romo's first extended outing was mild, as well as ambivalent, and reflected the dual nature of Romo's performance.

"Some good, but some bad," said Parcells, in stating what had been obvious to even the most casual fan.

Although Romo used different words to describe his play, he also spoke about being of two minds about his showing.

"I didn't get it done," acknowledged Romo, as he offered a direct and bottom line assessment of his performance. "But

I think that I showed that I have the ability to play in this league, and I hope I get another opportunity to prove that and build on what happened tonight."

The following day, Parcells announced that Romo would, indeed, be the starter for the Cowboys' following game, a Sunday night contest against the Panthers in Carolina.

"Any time you make a move of this magnitude, it's done with a lot of consideration," noted Parcells, in explaining that the changeover was more than merely a reaction to Bledsoe's bad first half against the Giants. "I've been thinking about it for some time. I'm hopeful that he might be able to do a couple of things for us. But he's got to be more careful with the ball."

Bledsoe, who had reacted angrily when he was taken out of the game, didn't feel any better about this decision.

"It's a very, very disappointing situation for me, but I can't go back and change it," said Bledsoe, who couldn't argue with the fact that he had thrown eight interceptions and lost a fumble in six games, while also being sacked 16 times, including 13 times in the past three games. "Obviously, I would like to be the guy still, and I really believe in my heart of hearts that I give us the best chance to win."

Jerry Jones, who thought that he had assembled a team with championship potential, was dismayed by the change, thinking that it might signify a giant step backwards for the Cowboys.

"I have to be honest and admit that I hadn't thought that we'd be sitting here after the sixth game, and needing to make an adjustment of this magnitude," said Jones, who later amended his comments to reflect a more hopeful outcome. "But I'm not dismissing the possibilities for this year. With the team we have and with the pluses that Tony could bring us, good things could still happen."

Owens, however, could hardly have been happier with the change, as he indicated that he already had a much better rapport with Romo than he had ever had with Bledsoe.

"On that touchdown pass that Tony threw to me against the Giants, I looked at him from across the formation, and he looked back at me and he knew what was going on," declared Owens. "It was just two players making a play."

Romo's parents were also thrilled to hear that their son was going to get a chance to start an NFL game and, maybe, just a little bit surprised.

"There's been times along the way when I was just relieved that he had gotten as far as he had," said Ramiro Romo. "I'd think, 'He did pretty good, he's a good kid, but he's not going to advance any further.' But you know what? He's proven me wrong every time. I'm not going to doubt him any more."

Ron Wolfe, the former Packers' general manager, who had made the trade that brought Brett Favre to Green Bay in 1992, also believed that Romo had the right stuff.

"He definitely has an ability to move the team," said Wolf. "He can improvise, he can move around, and he can throw the ball. Some quarterbacks can do all that and some can't. Tony Romo can. I know he had some rough moments against the Giants, but I was impressed with the fact that he kept throwing the football. That showed me that he hadn't lost confidence in himself. Now, we'll have to see if he can continue to improve and be successful."

8   TIME TO SHINE

Romo got off to a slow start against Carolina, and the Panthers, a team that many had thought would vie for the NFC title, jumped out to a 14-0 first-quarter lead, aided by an interception that the Panthers turned into their second score one play later. In situations like this, young and inexperienced quarterbacks often become unhinged and crumble under the challenge of having to be a playmaker. Romo, however, responded to the pressure by immediately leading the Cowboys down the field and connecting with tight end Jason Witten for a three-yard touchdown pass that cut Carolina's lead in half.

The powerful Panthers' defense stiffened, however, and the Cowboys, who had tacked on a pair of field goals, still found themselves on the short end of a 14-13 score early in the fourth quarter. Then, the Dallas defense, which had stifled the Panthers' offense since the third quarter, created three fourth-quarter turnovers, and Romo rewarded their efforts by turning each of the takeaways into scoring drives, as the Cowboys rallied for a 35-14 win.

"The way he came back and got us a win let everyone know that he had a bright future ahead of him," said Jason Witten, who, right after the first-quarter interception, had told Romo that it was a long game, and that he should stay calm and focused. "He showed that he had the ability and the toughness that is needed to be successful in this league."

Although Romo, who completed 26 of 34 passes for 270

yards, is among the most modest of athletes, he couldn't contain the excitement that he felt in turning his first NFL start into a rousing success.

"We went against a good team," said Romo, sounding as bubbly as a glass of Champagne. "On the road, against a team with a great defense."

But he also communicated the sense that he wasn't going to be overwhelmed by his situation, and that the future would be better than the present.

"The one thing is, at each level I've had to figure out what it takes to get good at that level," said Romo, sounding as if he was making a promise. "It just takes a little time. I thought the opportunity was going to happen sometime, and I knew when it did, that I better be ready."

And while Romo was relishing his first sweet taste of NFL success, he wasn't about to take it for granted.

"I'm going to watch film," said Romo, in answer to what he planned to do in the way of celebration. "You know as well as I do that you can go from the penthouse to the outhouse in a heartbeat."

Roy Wittke, who had done so much to develop Romo's talent and tenaciousness at the college level, had watched the game on television, and was almost as gleeful as his star pupil.

"He had a tremendous attitude and approach," said Wittke. "He knew if he continued to work hard and prepared himself that he would get the opportunity. The work and preparation led to him gaining more confidence in his ability to play at that level, which isn't all that surprising when you stop to think about it. He's always been the type of guy who, regardless of the situation, managed to get the job done. I don't think there's any reason to believe that he won't do it again in Dallas."

Romo's play had also seemed to ignite the entire team, including Witten, who had six catches for 80 yards, and Terrell Owens, who snared nine passes for 107 yards, both of which were season highs through game seven.

"We just came together as a team tonight and it's about time," said Owens. "We're finally getting to where we need to be."

Even the usually dour Parcells was caught up by the sudden change in the team's temperament.

"You know, we haven't been having a lot of fun here, but they're having fun right now" said Parcells in his post-game news conference, while also offering guarded approval of Romo's play. "He has guts, I'll say that. He takes his swings. He's not standing there with the bat on his shoulders. I like that. I thought he did a pretty good job, but we've got some things to work on. He made some plays on impulse and improvisation, but you can't play the game like that in this league. You have to learn how to play. I'm not counting on any chickens."

Romo realized that he had to refine his skills and cut down on his mistakes if he was going to establish himself in the NFL and earn the trust of his coach.

"I know he's going to be on my case," said Romo. "He's like that with everyone, and I know that he expects—demands—a lot of out of me, but that's good."

The following week, the Cowboys were on the road against Washington, and found themselves locked in a 19-19 tie with only 31 seconds left to play. With the ball on their own 39-yard line, Romo went to work and quickly led the team down to the Washington 17-yard line, his 28-yard strike to Jason Witten perfectly positioning Mike Vanderjagt for a game-winning 35-yard field goal with just six ticks left on the clock. But the kick was blocked and recovered by Washington, and their kicker, Nick Novak, drove the ball through the uprights to give Washington an improbable 22-19 win on the game's final play.

Romo, who had completed 24-of-36 passes for 284 yards, two touchdowns and no interceptions, wasn't consoled by his personal stat line or willing to blame Terrell Owens, who had dropped what would have been a 74-yard touchdown pass.

"No, I don't feel good," said Romo. "I'm not here to put up numbers. I'm here to help this team win. In this league, it's very hard to keep bouncing around like this. We'll bounce back, but it's frustrating that we didn't come up with a win today."

While Parcells was also stunned by the sudden reversal of fortune, he was pleased by the way Romo was handling himself.

"I can't ask for any more than what I've seen these first two games," said Parcells. "He won one game and had the team in position to win the second one. You can't ask the player to do any more than that."

The Cowboys went on the road again the following week, but this time they came away with a 27-10 win over the Arizona Cardinals, with Romo again leading the way. In only his third game as the Dallas starter, Romo was almost flawless, as he completed 20-of-29 passes for 308 yards and a pair of touchdowns. The second scoring pass resulted from Romo's ability to read defenses and to change the play at the line of scrimmage. When he saw the Arizona cornerback come up to play bump-and-run against Owens, he signaled T.O. to abort the short hook pattern that had been called in the huddle and, instead, to run a deep fly route down the left sideline. Then, after a play fake, he hit Owens in stride for the game-clinching 51-yard touchdown connection.

"When we made the quarterback change, my first thought was that a wheel had come off the bus," said Jerry Jones. "But I didn't anticipate the poise and level of execution that Tony has demonstrated. It looks like as he evolves, we'll have a guy who we can win with right now, and who will be really good in the future."

Although they hadn't had much trouble in clocking the clueless Cardinals, their immediate future looked less promising, however, because the Cowboys' next game was against the undefeated Indianapolis Colts, who came into Texas Stadium with the league's top-rated quarterback, Peyton Manning, its highest-scoring offense, and a 9-0 record.

In the first half, however, it was the defenses that were dominant, as the Colts took a 7-0 lead into the locker room. The Cowboys' offense remained stagnant throughout the third quarter, although linebacker Kevin Burnett put Dallas on the scoreboard when he picked off a Manning pass and took it into the end zone for a game-tying touchdown.

After the Colts retook the lead, 14-7, Romo was finally able to ignite the Cowboys' offense in the fourth quarter, starting with a 15-play, 68-yard scoring drive that was capped by a five-yard burst into the end zone by running back Marion Barber. Then, with the score tied and less than 10 minutes left to play, Romo directed the Cowboys on an 80-yard drive, starting with a 19-yard completion to wide receiver Terry Glenn, who had run a quick-hitting slant pattern. Romo and the speedy Glenn, who had six catches in the game, followed that reception with a 33-yard pass play on which Glenn faked the slant route, then cut back to the outside, snared the pass and raced down the right sideline until he was pushed out of bounds at the Colts' 28-yard line.

After a 15-yard screen pass to running back Julius Jones, who dragged Colts' linebacker Cato June down to the one, Barber banged the ball into the end zone for his second score of the game, as the Cowboys toppled the Colts' run at perfection, 21-14.

"Romo's been the coolest dude around here for awhile," said Cowboys' inside linebacker Bradie James. "The outside world didn't know that, but what he's been doing in the games are the same things that we've always seen him do in practice. It may be brand-new to everyone else, but it's old hat to us."

The win upped the Cowboys' record to 6-4, which put them into a first place tie with the Giants in the NFC East, and made a trip to the playoffs seem a much likelier possibility than it had a few weeks earlier.

"That was one of the biggest wins we've had here in a while, but it won't be much if we don't carry it over to our next game," said Romo. "Beating the Colts certainly helped our confidence, but whenever you get to a point where you feel that you're good enough, then you're already going backwards. We need to prepare the same as we did last week and be ready to go."

They had to get ready in a hurry, because next up for the Cowboys was a Thursday afternoon Thanksgiving Day contest against the Tampa Bay Buccaneers. The short week didn't do anything to derail the Cowboys' express, however, as Romo riddled the Bucs' defense for 306 passing yards and five scoring passes, while Dallas romped to a 38-10 win in front of their hometown fans.

Jerry Jones was ecstatic with the way the team was performing, which reminded him of past glory days in Dallas.

"Frankly, in these back-to-back wins, we look the best that we've looked in 10 years," said the Dallas owner, apparently not even counting the team's win over hapless Arizona. "They are making a championship effort."

While Jones only seemed to see blue skies, Parcells tried to remind people that neither the team nor its electric young quarterback were finished products.

"Look, he's playing well, and he has a great attitude," said Parcells, who can always spot the dark lining in the puffiest white cloud. "But we've got a ways to go here, so put the anointing oil away. We haven't won anything yet."

Parcells' realistic appraisal didn't dent Romo's confidence or provoke a dissent from him.

"I think I do have some faults," said Romo, who had an NFL-best 110.8 quarterback rating. "I've got to work on some things and get better. Believe me, I haven't arrived yet."

9   STREET PLAYER

The basis for the reservations that Parcells had voiced was illustrated in the first half of the Cowboys' next game, when Romo threw a pair of interceptions against the Giants, the same team that had picked him off three times when he had replaced Bledsoe in the second half of the teams' earlier meeting.

Although Romo didn't throw any more interceptions in the second half, he didn't get the offense in gear until the middle of the fourth quarter. With the teams tied at 13-13, Romo led the Cowboys on a 12-play, 66-yard drive, which was capped by Marion Barber's 7-yard burst with 3:33 left to play. It was Barber's second rushing touchdown of the game and his 11th score of the season.

The Giants' offense, which had been held in check all game, suddenly sprang to life, as Eli Manning hit six straight completions, the final one being a 5-yard game-tying scoring pass to Plaxico Burress with 1:12 left in regulation time.

"That's the way it is in this league," said Romo. "Every team has playmakers who are capable of making good things happen quickly. When they tied it up, we knew what we had to do, and I think we were all pretty confident that we would get it done."

On the first play from scrimmage after the Giants' score, Romo faded back, slid to his left to avoid the rush, and then threw a 42-yard dart to Jason Witten that moved the ball down to the Giants' 26-yard line. Four plays later, Martin

Gramatica, who had replaced Vanderjagt as the team's field goal kicker, split the uprights to give the Cowboys a last-second 23-20 win at Giants Stadium.

"If I've got one drive, I want Tony as my quarterback," said Witten. "That's a bold statement, but that's the way I feel. He's so competitive and wants to win so badly. He certainly didn't play his best game, but he showed his poise by coming up big in crunch time."

Romo, who had been named the NFC Offensive Player of the Month for November, his first month as a starter, was also supremely secure in his ability to deliver the goods, especially when a game was on the line.

"I'm always confident when I'm out there," said Romo, who had led the Cowboys to a 5-1 record since his installation as the starting quarterback, while completing 67.8 percent of his passes and compiling an NFL-best 102.4 quarterback rating. "In the fourth quarter, with the chance to win, that's what you play this game for."

Romo's upbeat attitude and exuberance, his obvious love of competition, his courage in the face of adversity and his enthusiastic response to challenges had energized the entire team.

"He has given us a rebirth, provided us with more positive energy," said linebacker Bradie James, not just echoing what his teammates felt, but also expressing the views of football fans throughout the Dallas area. "The thing is, he just has this swagger about him. It's not cockiness, but a sense of confidence that just radiates off of him. You just have to love him."

Jerry Jones, who had been so dubious about the quarterback change back in October, had done a full 180, and climbed up on the Romo bandwagon.

"All of a sudden we've won five of six," said Jones. "The same coach has been here. The other players are the same. What's the difference? The obvious explanation is that we've got a quarterback that can make things gel."

RomoMania wasn't just a Dallas phenomenon or even limited to teammates and fans. Romo's sudden and unexpected emergence as a budding superstar had even caught the attention and admiration of other players in the league.

"It's such a feel good story, because he had to scrape and scratch and overcome a lot of skeptics," said Chicago Bears' quarterback Rex Grossman, who had been a first round pick in the 2003 draft, and became the team's starter the following season. "He obviously deserves this opportunity because he worked so hard to get it, and now he's making the most of it."

As usual, Parcells was a whole lot less euphoric in his praise of Romo than anyone else.

"Well, he didn't have his best day, but he got us down the field when it counted," said Parcells, speaking about the win over the Giants, but making a face more suitable to a patient coming out of oral surgery than anything you might expect from a coach who had just seen his team defeat a division rival on the road, in the literal last second of play. "And that's all I'm going to say about him."

Later in the week, Parcells was a bit more generous in his praise of Romo. Even though he knew that six games wasn't nearly enough time to properly evaluate a quarterback, Parcells couldn't help but admire the intensity with which Romo plays the game, even comparing him to former Giants' Hall of Famer Lawrence Taylor, who many people consider to be the greatest linebacker of all time.

"He's like a street player; he really is," said Parcells, referring to Romo's ability to scramble and create on the fly, which isn't a style of play that Parcells normally endorses, let alone tolerates. "He plays as though he's in the park. That's the kind of kid he is. He enjoys that aspect of the game and he's a competitor, and it's not hard to keep a player that lives to compete. It's like when I had Lawrence in New York; just show him the competition and he was ready to go for it."

Parcells, however, wasn't quite ready to nominate Romo for induction in Canton. He felt that all the enthusiasts were getting way ahead of themselves in their praise of his young and inexperienced quarterback, and that all the people delivering the hype were in need of a reality check. He realized that Romo was on a nice run, but he also knew that he hadn't come close to crossing the finish line.

"Trust me, the challenge for Tony isn't over," said Parcells, who could recite a long list of short-term hotshots who had quickly flamed out and faded away. "He's just at the starting gate. He's still taking baby steps. Let's not put him in the Hall of Fame just yet."

10   STARTLED IN SEATTLE

The people who thought that Parcells' reservations had been overdone had their eyes opened the following week when Romo completed less than half of his pass attempts and threw a pair of interceptions, as the New Orleans Saints marched into Texas Stadium and manhandled the Cowboys, 42-17.

"It's like I've been telling you, he still has a lot to learn," Parcells told the assembled media. "He hasn't even played a half a season yet, so it shouldn't come as a surprise that he's going to make some mistakes. But I'm also confident that he'll get back to doing the good things that we saw in earlier games."

The loss and his poor play stung Romo, whose usual sunny disposition seemed shrouded in dark clouds. But he was determined to put the experience behind him and get ready for the next game.

"As soon as I leave here today, I'm going to do my best to let it go because, if you hold on too long, it winds up having a negative effect on your next game," explained Romo, who was dealing with the first real set-back in his seven games as the Cowboys' starter. "Being as competitive as I am, it may take me a while, but as soon I get to practice, I'll let it go."

It appeared that Romo and his teammates might be singing the blues the following week, however, as Michael Vick torched the Dallas secondary for four touchdown passes on four consecutive possessions straddling the first and second halves, and the Atlanta Falcons took a 28-21 lead at the Georgia Dome. Vick also scrambled for 56 yards, upping his rushing total for the season to 990 yards, which broke the record for a quarterback that had been set by former Chicago Bears' signal-caller Bobby Douglas in 1972 when he rushed for 968 yards.

Just when it looked as though Vick couldn't be stopped, the Dallas defense shut him down, while the Romo-led offense scored the final 17 points in the game to give the Cowboys a 38-28 victory. The win, which gave the Cowboys a 9-5 record, assured them of having consecutive winning seasons for the first time since 1995-96 and, more importantly, it guaranteed them a spot in the playoffs for the first time since 2003.

"I don't think people realize how important this game was," said Romo, who sounded relieved as well as exuberant. "This was the biggest game we've had all year."

Everyone in the Dallas locker room, including Jerry Jones and Parcells, seemed elated about the team's ability to bounce back from their shellacking by the Saints with their late charge against the Falcons.

"I think my team showed a lot of guts tonight," said Parcells. "The defense settled down and the offense drove the ball for three consecutive scores in the second half. Naturally, I'm happy about a game like that."

The good feelings continued through the middle of the week, when it was announced that four Cowboys, including Romo, had been selected to play in the Pro Bowl, the NFL's annual All-Star game, which is played in Hawaii the week following the Super Bowl.

"It's exciting, and it means a lot to me that the players

and coaches voted for me," said Romo, who had compiled a 6-2 record in his eight starts, and had thrown for 2,400 yards, 16 touchdowns and only 10 interceptions, while leading the NFC with a 98.4 quarterback rating and a 66.3 completion percentage. "I just really appreciate all the people who voted for me."

But the good feelings that the Cowboys had, disappeared like spring snow as they finished the season with losses at home to the Eagles, who passed them in the standings and went on to take the division title, and, more devastatingly, the Detroit Lions, who had come into Dallas with a 2-13 record.

After the 23-7 loss to the Eagles, in which Romo completed only 14 of 29 passes for 142 yards and threw two interceptions, Parcells put the Cowboys' immediate future into perspective.

"I told the team that they can either be judged by this game or they can come back ready to go next week and try to compete for a championship, which they're going to have the opportunity to do," explained Parcells. "I think we'll know next week at this time which way we're going to go."

With Parcells looking at the Lions game as a predictor for how the team would fare in the playoffs, he couldn't have had much faith in the future, because Detroit, which had had trouble scoring points all season long, defeated Dallas, 39-31.

"I can't tell you how disappointed I am, I really can't," said Parcells, who was stunned by the unexpected turn of events. "This is a low point for me. I'm disappointed because I just wanted my team to be playing better right now."

Although the Dallas defense, which had become porous

in the later part of the season, bore a major responsibility for the loss, another Jekyll and Hyde performance by Romo also hurt the Cowboys' cause. While he threw for 321 yards and a pair of touchdowns, he was also guilty of throwing an interception and losing the football on two of his four fumbles.

"Tony made some outstanding improvisational plays, and he just missed scoring a touchdown on our last play, which would have put us in position to tie the game with a 2-point conversion," said Parcells, while explaining that the more times a gambler rolls the dice, the more likely it is that he'll crap out. "He did that four or five times today, but those plays never offset what the bad plays cost you. I don't want to take away his creativity, but he has to learn when to take a risk and when not to."

As stunned as he was by the loss, Romo was more interested in looking ahead to a possibly rosy future than he was in dwelling on the team's dismal showing against Detroit, the worst team in the NFC.

"As bad I feel right now, I'll be able to smile tomorrow because we're in the playoffs and we have a chance to win the whole thing," said Romo. "Only 12 teams have a chance to do that. From that perspective, that's all I can ask."

The Cowboys traveled to Seattle to play the Seahawks in a wild-card match-up between a pair of 9-7 teams, each of which was hoping to redeem a season that had begun with higher aspirations. For Romo, the return to Qwest Field brought back pleasant memories of the first game of the pre-season, when Parcells had let him play the entire contest, and he had shown just how far he had come in his development as a quarterback.

"Individually, that was probably every bit as important

as any game I've ever played in," said Romo, before he turned his attention to the playoff showdown. "For us, we just have to play without turning the ball over. Play mistake-free football and just do what we do best."

In the end, however, it was miscues that brought the Cowboys' season to an excruciatingly painful end.

The game had developed into a hard-fought, low-scoring, defensive struggle, with neither team enjoying more than a four point lead until the Cowboys, playing catch-up, scored a late-third-quarter touchdown on a kickoff return, and then added an early-fourth-quarter field goal to take a 20-13 lead with 10:15 left in the game. But the Seahawks were able to turn a Terry Glenn fumble into a safety, and then added a touchdown on their next possession to retake the lead, 21-20, after failing to score a 2-point conversion attempt.

With their season on the line and only 4:24 left on the clock, Romo led the Cowboys from their own 28-yard line down to the Seattle two, facing a fourth-and-one with 1:19 left to play. Parcells sent Gramatica into the game to kick a chip-shot field goal from the 19-yard line, which would have vaulted the Cowboys back into the lead. But Romo fumbled the snap and, with no other option available, tried to run the ball into the end zone, or at least to the 1-yard line, which would have given the Cowboys a first down. Before he could reach either of his goals, however, Seattle defensive back Jordan Babineaux wrestled Romo down at the 2-yard line.

The Cowboys had one last-second attempt to snatch victory away from Seattle after the Seahawks had to punt the ball back to the Cowboys, but Romo's final desperate fling fell incomplete in the end zone.

"I didn't get it down, and I cost us the game," said Romo,

speaking about his fumble on the aborted field goal try. "It hurts real bad right now to think about it because I know how hard the guys in the locker room worked to get us into position to win this game. I feel disappointed because I let the guys down today, and the fans and the organization, too. That was my fault. I cost the Dallas Cowboys a playoff win, and it's going to sit with me for a long time."

11 TAKING THE NEXT STEP

During the course of the next several weeks, Romo, with the support of his teammates, especially Witten and Owens, began to let go of the anguish that he felt about his fumble and started to use the painful experience to motivate himself for the 2007 season.

"If you're a competitor, it's always going to be lurking someplace in the background," said Romo. "I know when I'm lifting weights or throwing the ball at night at the training complex I have an extra little chip on my shoulder that pushes me to work harder. I mean, I always work hard, but that play has given me an added incentive."

A few weeks after the Cowboys' playoff loss, Parcells announced his retirement from coaching, and a veteran NFL coach, Wade Phillips, replaced him. Also joining the staff, as the team's new offensive coordinator, was Jason Garrett, who very quickly came to appreciate Romo's serious work ethic.

"He has a strong desire to be a great quarterback and he's willing to work really hard to achieve that goal," said Garrett, who was Troy Aikman's backup with the Cowboys from 1993-1999. "He comes to practice and gets really dialed in. If he keeps working like this, lots of good things are going to happen for him and the Dallas Cowboys."

By sheer coincidence, the Cowboys opened their 2007 campaign against the Giants at Texas Stadium, the same opponent and venue where Romo had received his first real playing time the previous year. But the fact that the NFL had scheduled the contest as the first nationally-televised Sunday night game of the season was, in part, a deliberate choice to highlight Romo as an emerging star. Although he had come so far in so short a time since that game against the Giants in Dallas, Romo wasn't about to rest on his laurels.

"At the end of the day, everybody has to come out and prove they're good all over again," said Romo. "Each year brings a whole new set of challenges, a new proving ground to test your ability to help your team win. That's what it's all about."

Then, Romo went out and put on a show by throwing four touchdown passes and scrambling in for a fifth score, as he led the Cowboys to a 45-35 win. The final score was somewhat deceiving, however, because Eli Manning had also brought his *A* game, and the contest wasn't secured until late in the fourth quarter, when Romo threw a 51-yard touchdown pass to Sam Hurd, who was filling in for the injured Terry Glenn. The 80 points were the most ever scored in the 90-game history between the two division rivals.

"It was beginning to look like a basketball score," said a smiling Romo, who threw for a career-high 345 yards on only 15 completions. "It's great to start the season off with any kind of win, but even more so because we were able to step up late in the game."

After a slow start the following week, in Miami, the Cowboys won handily, 37-20, thanks in no small part to the generosity of the Dolphins, who turned the ball over five times, including four interception tosses by their quarterback, Trent Green. The Cowboys found themselves involved in another low-scoring first half the following week, as well, as a suffocating Chicago defense held them to a single field goal. But they piled up the points in the second half and battered the Bears, 34-10. All of the Cowboys' skill-position players delivered big-time, including Barber, who ran for 102 yards, and Owens, who caught a pair of touchdown passes and racked up 145 passing yards on eight receptions, which allowed him to become only the 14th player in league history to surpass the 12,000-yard mark.

"I think the journey that we're going on has been a fun trip so far," said Romo, who threw for 329 yards and a pair of third-quarter touchdowns that put the Cowboys in front to stay. "We have an explosive offense, and I think it's going to be an exciting ride for the rest of the year."

The Cowboys continued their joyride by demolishing the Rams, 35-7, behind a trio of touchdown passes and a 15-yard scoring scamper by Romo, who was named the NFC Offensive Player of the Month for September, after leading the Cowboys to a perfect 4-0 record.

But the magical tour seemed to come to a crashing halt the following week in a Monday night game in Buffalo, as Romo fumbled once and was picked off *five* times, which helped stake the Bills to a 24-12 fourth quarter lead. Just when it seemed the game was lost, however, Romo led the Cowboys on a trio of fourth-quarter scoring drives, including two in the final 20 seconds. The last drive began after the recovery of an onside kick, and it ended when rookie Nick Folk split the uprights with no time left on the clock, which allowed Dallas to squeeze out a stunning 25-24 win.

"I haven't been around anything like this, and I've been in the league for 31 years," said Wade Phillips.

"That's a sign of a resilient team," said Romo who, despite his misadventures, still managed to throw another pair of touchdown passes and set a Cowboys' single-season record by throwing for 300 yards for the fourth time with 11 games left to play. "Aside from me, the rest of the team played an outstanding game. They dug me out of it."

Although there was a great deal of truth to Romo's self-criticism, his teammates saw the other side of the coin, as well.

"During the game, I tried to say something to him just because we're buddies, but he doesn't need coddling," said Witten, who turned nine catches into 103 yards and a touchdown. "He has confidence in who he is and what he does, and I think that shows at the end of games. As bad as he played for most of the game, without him we're not even in it."

The next game for the Cowboys was against the New England Patriots, a schedule-maker's dream, which featured a match-up between a pair of undefeated teams, who were also the league's two highest-ranked offenses. Both teams featured a cast of high-profile performers, including the Patriots' passing-game duo of quarterback Tom Brady and wide receiver Randy Moss, who were playing at the top of their games. Fan interest in the contest was so intense that scalpers in Dallas were reportedly able to resell tickets for more than a thousand dollars each.

The Cowboys managed to hang tough through the first three quarters of the game, which was something that no other team had been able to do against New England. But then the Patriots piled on 17 fourth-quarter points to win going away, 49-27, behind Brady's five touchdown passes.

"Tom's obviously really special and he's tough to beat," said Romo, who threw a couple of touchdown passes but was otherwise held in check by the Pats' defense. "He's taken that team to the next level."

After the loss to the Patriots, the Cowboys quickly regrouped and went on to win seven straight games, and Romo and Owens went on to become the most feared passing duo in the NFC. During the winning streak, the Cowboys beat the Giants for a second time, and the Green Bay Packers, in a game that was hyped in much the same way as their earlier face-off against the Patriots.

The game against the Packers involved a match-up of co-conference leaders, who came into the contest with identical 10-1 records. Making the game even more dramatic was the fact that Romo, the new kid on the quarterback block, would be going up against the team he had cheered for as a boy and sharing a field with Brett Favre, the near-legendary quarterback of the Packers. Unfortunately, the nearly indestructible Favre, who holds the all-time record for consecutive starts by a quarterback—as well of most of the league's major passing records—was injured in the first half and forced to leave the game. But the thrill of the occasion was one that will stay with Romo.

"When I went on the field, I realized how electric the atmosphere was," said Romo, who threw for 309 yards and four touchdowns. "It was exciting to go against a 10-1 team and the one that I had rooted for when I was growing up. I looked around and thought, 'This is pretty neat. This is why you play sports. You want to play in games like this, because they really get your juices flowing, and you want to show that you're a decent player.'"

The four touchdown passes upped Romo's season total to 33, breaking the club record of 29 that had been set by Danny White in 1983, and he tied another franchise mark by throwing a touchdown pass in his 16th consecutive game.

"I would say that Tony has had, by far, the best season

that any Dallas quarterback has ever had," said Troy Aikman, who was at the game along with Roger Staubach, the Cowboys' other Hall of Fame signal-caller. "You don't have to be a rocket scientist to know that."

In the last game of the Cowboys' winning streak, Romo rallied the team for a pair of fourth quarter touchdowns, the first on a short burst by Barber, his third of the game, and the second by Witten, who pulled in a 16-yarder with 18 ticks left on the clock.

Although the Cowboys lost two of their final three games, they still finished the regular season with a 13-3 record for only the second time in franchise history, and they also captured their first NFC East title since 1998. The team's accomplishments were reflected in the fact that 12 of them—a franchise record—were selected to play in the Pro Bowl, including Barber, Witten, Owens, Romo and three of their five offensive linemen.

"We had a tremendous year," declared Phillips. "We accomplished all of our goals for the regular season, but the playoffs are the second season, and we're looking forward to them."

The Cowboy's opponent in the divisional round was the Giants, who had knocked off Tampa Bay in a wild-card game, while Dallas, which had a bye-week because of their first-place finish, was able to take a week off. Although the Cowboys had defeated the Giants twice in the regular season and had finished three games ahead of them, the visitors were coming into Texas Stadium under a full head of steam after nearly ending New England's perfect season the week before they beat the Bucs.

The Giants continued their recent good play by striking on the game's first possession, when wide receiver Amani

Toomer took a short pass from Eli Manning, broke a couple of tackles, and romped into the end zone for a 52-yard score. The Cowboys answered back on their second possession, with Barber eating up huge chunks of yardage on a 96-yard drive, which Romo capped with a 5-yard touchdown pass to Owens just seconds into the second quarter.

After the Giants were forced to punt, Romo led the Cowboys on another long drive, keeping the Giants' defense off-balance by mixing the running game with passing plays, and finishing it with a handoff to Barber, who burst in for the score from the 1-yard line.

The Cowboys were pumped, thinking that, with under a minute left in the quarter, they would be taking a lead into the locker room. But, after the kickoff, Manning's passing quickly led the Giants down the field and, with just seven seconds left in the half, he connected with Toomer for another score and the Giants went into the break on a high note, while Dallas went to their locker room on a decided down beat.

Despite their disappointment at the Giants' late score, the Cowboys took the opening kickoff of the second half and went on a 14-play drive that ended with Nick Folk kicking a 34-yard field goal and giving Dallas the lead, 17-14.

After both teams were forced to punt, the Giants wound up with excellent field position, and Manning exploited the opportunity by directing the team on a short drive that ended with Brandon Jacobs, their mega-sized tailback, busting over right guard for a touchdown that put Dallas on the short side of a 21-17 score with 13:33 left to play.

Although the Cowboys would have three more possessions in the final quarter, Romo wasn't able to pull any rabbits out of his hat on that particular day, and his final desperate pass of the season sailed into the end zone, where it was snatched out of the air by Giants' cornerback, R.W. McQuarters.

In the immediate aftermath of the loss, Romo sat with his head between his knees, his voice barely rising above a whisper, as he felt the pain of being bounced out of the playoffs, and losing the dream of a Super Bowl that had seemed to be very reachable.

"It hurts right now," said Romo, who was 18-of-36 for 201 yards, a single touchdown and the interception. "It's tough right now."

But even in the midst of his despair, Romo had the strength to count his blessings and appreciate his circumstances.

"I've grown up, in the sense that I know that things don't always, or even usually, work out perfectly, so even though we didn't accomplish our goal of reaching the Super Bowl, I appreciate what we've done and where I'm at," said Romo. "I wouldn't trade this season with these guys and this coaching staff for anything. It was the most fun that I've ever had."

Although Romo has suffered through playoff losses in both of his two seasons as a starter, Wade Phillips put those losses in their proper perspective.

"I can't believe in a quarterback more than I believe in Tony," said Phillips, who pointed out that Hall of Fame quarterback John Elway didn't win a Super Bowl until his final two years in the NFL. "This is a young guy who has played for only a year and a half, and is getting better and better. He had a tremendous season in 2007, and that will carry over into future seasons."

Romo, who threw for more yards and touchdowns in a singe season than any other Dallas quarterback ever had and who had signed a long-term contract extension in the middle of the season, was also able to look and see even brighter tomorrows.

"I think this organization is definitely headed in the right direction," said Romo, the boy from Burlington who had overcome so many odds to even make it into the NFL. "I think we'll be back playing in playoff games in the future, with the chance to win a lot of them."

TONY ROMO

Born: April 21, 1980, in San Diego, California
Height: 6-2   Weight: 224
College: Eastern Illinois Round drafted: Not drafted NFL Seasons: 4

CAREER STATS

Att.	Comp.	Pct.	Yards	TD	Int.	QB Rating
857	555	64.8	7,114	55	32	96.5

65

BEN ROETHLISBERGER

Born: March 2, 1981, in Lima, Ohio
Height: 6-5   Weight: 241
College: Miami (Ohio)   Round drafted: First   NFL Seasons: 4

CAREER STATS

Att.	Comp.	Pct.	Yards	TD	Int.	QB Rating
1,436	908	64.8	11,673	84	54	92.5

1   ROTTY

Ben Roethlisberger, the only child of Ken and Ida, was born March 2, 1982, in Lima, Ohio. Eighteen months later, his parents were divorced and Roethlisberger wound up living with his father, while spending alternate weekends with his mother.

Ken had been a standout high school quarterback and baseball player, who went to Georgia Tech on a football scholarship. After an injury ended his football career, he switched back to baseball and played shortstop for the Yellow Jackets. It was his love of sports that brought him to a local lunchtime pick-up basketball game, where he met a woman named Brenda, who had played college basketball. The meeting was short and violent, as Brenda cut through the lane and accidentally knocked Ken on his backside. Despite that rough introduction, the two of them fell in love and eventually married and Brenda became Ben's stepmother.

Although children often suffer in the aftermath of a divorce, Roethlisberger seems to be one of the lucky ones who have managed to survive the rupture without any ill effects. In large part, that's likely due to the fact that he was loved and cared for by his dad and Brenda, and by his biological mother, as well. It also helped that he seemed to be mature beyond his years.

"When I came into the picture, Ben and his dad had spent a lot of time together, doing grown-up things," recalled Brenda, who is a part-time yoga teacher. "Then I came along, and we did more grown-up things. He was used to hanging around with adults and I think he just started to act like one."

One day, when Roethlisberger was eight years old, he was shooting hoops at his house, waiting for Ida to pick him up and take him out for some ice cream. But, on the way to see her son, Ida was critically injured in a car accident and fell into a coma. She died three weeks later, without ever regaining consciousness.

"Ben has been through a lot," said Brenda. "But he's shown courage and made something of himself, despite those hardships, and I think that's one of the reasons that he's become so popular."

Roethlisberger has been able to stay so positive, despite suffering through events that have traumatized so many other people, because he always felt nourished and secure within his family.

"I like the way I was raised," said Roethlisberger, who calls Brenda *Mom*. "My parents taught me the values of hard work, dedication and loyalty. Those are the qualities that are important to me, and they're also the values I bring to sports."

When Roethlisberger was 10 years old, the family, which had grown to include Ken and Brenda's daughter, Carlee, moved to the city of Findlay, Ohio, which is about 34 miles northeast of Lima and 180 miles west of Cleveland. Findlay, with a population of about 40,000 people, has a small-town, suburban look and feel to it, with, mostly, one-family homes set on well-kept lawns.

The home that the Roethlisbergers moved into is a modest, three-bedroom red-brick ranch house, which sits on a quiet, pretty street. A large maple tree dominates the front yard and carefully landscaped plantings and shrubs surround the home.

"The backyard was large enough for us to play lots of games," recalled, Ken, as he stood in front of a backboard in the driveway. "We always spent a lot of time together as a family. You only have your kids for such a short time."

For Brenda, the relatively small size of the house worked to the family's advantage, although one gets the sense that this family could just as easily have lived in a 20-room mansion without it having any negative effect on their relationships.

"The house is small, but it has kept our family close," said Brenda. "Everything has always happened in the family room and kitchen, or in the front and back yards."

"As long as I can remember, all the way through my high school years, we ate dinner at home every night, unless there was a sporting event, and lots of times we'd eat breakfast together, too," said Roethlisberger. "That's why I think my family means so much to me, and why I have such a good family background."

When Roethlisberger joined the Findlay fifth-grade football team, he told the coach, Mike Iriti, that he would like to play running back. That was fine with Iriti, whose son, Michael, was the team's quarterback. But it didn't take long for the coach to decide to shuffle his lineup.

"In the second game, we ran a trick play, a flea-flicker, and Ben wound up winging the ball 25 yards down the field and hitting Mike right in stride," said Iriti, smacking his hands together for emphasis. "I told them, 'From now on, Ben, you're the quarterback, and Mike, you're the receiver.'"

Even then, it was obvious to Iriti that Roethlisberger had been gifted with great athleticism and an unusual level of poise, especially for one so young.

"You don't expect a kid to make every play, but Ben always seemed to make things work," said Iriti, who coached Roethlisberger for two years. "He has a lot of natural talent and an ability to stay calm and focused in situations that would rattle most other people. Some kids just rise above the rest, and Ben was one of those."

Roethlisberger continued to demonstrate his exceptional athletic ability at Findlay High School, where he was a three-sport star. Like his father, Roethlisberger was a fine baseball player and shortstop, and in his junior year he hit for a .300 average while earning all-district honors, but then he decided not to play the following year. The two sports in which he really excelled, however, were basketball, which was his first love, and football.

He was such a good basketball player that he was able to make the varsity in his freshman year. As the Trojans' point guard, he ran the offense, much like a quarterback does, and in his senior year he averaged 26.5 points, nine rebounds and five assists per game, while also serving as the team captain.

"You always wanted the ball in his hands, because he could control the tempo of the game, and it always seemed as if he had eyes in the back of his head," recalled Mike Iriti. "He was a good shooter, but with his body size—he was a bit lanky, but he stood 6-3 or 6-4—he could also post-up against defenders, and it was game over."

Roethlisberger still holds the school's career scoring record for boys that he set in 2000, but his sister Carlee, who now plays for the University of Oklahoma Sooners, easily surpassed her big brother's total, and is the current overall record holder.

"There's a direct parallel between the way he plays

football and the way he played basketball," said Jerry Snodgrass, who coached the Trojans' basketball team. "He was a little unorthodox with his shot, but he had an uncanny ability to score. It didn't matter where he was on the court—inside, outside, he'd throw the ball from anywhere and he'd usually score. He loves the sport so much that I'd bet that if he's driving around Pittsburgh and sees a game going on in a park, that it would take all his will power to not stop his car and try to join in."

Ironically, Roethlisberger didn't get to play quarterback for the varsity until his senior season at Findlay. He was the signal-caller for the junior varsity in his sophomore season, because Cliff Hite, the Trojans' coach, felt that his son, Ryan, who was a year ahead of Roethlisberger, was the better quarterback. The following season the coach kept his son at quarterback for his senior season, and played Roethlisberger at wide receiver.

"Some people say that I was a knucklehead," said Cliff Hite. "One day I may become as infamous as the coach who cut Michael Jordan from his high school basketball team.

"It wasn't as if I didn't try to do it the other way. We went through seven-on-seven drills during the summer, and my son would always throw the ball to Ben and he would always catch it. He was, like 6-4, and the guys trying to cover him were more like 5-9; it was a total mismatch. Ryan wasn't a tall, go-up-and-get-it kind of guy. So what kind of receiver was he going to be?"

Roethlisberger wasn't happy with the coach's decision, but he put his disappointment behind him and did the best that he could as a wide receiver.

"At the time, I was upset because I felt that I should have been the quarterback," said Roethlisberger. "But I can look back at it now from where I'm at and realize that it all worked out in the end."

No one will ever know how the Trojans' season would have worked out if Roethlisberger had been their quarterback and Ryan Hite, who was the team's fastest runner, had played wide receiver. What is known, however, is that Hite set a school record for total offense, by passing for 1,732 yards and rushing for 313 yards, while leading the team to a 6-4 record, as Findlay captured its first league championship in 15 years. Roethlisberger, meanwhile, did a fine job as a wide out, snaring 57 passes, for 757 yards and seven touchdowns. He also passed for two TDs on trick plays and, perhaps, became a better quarterback in the long run by gaining a view of the game from a receiver's perspective.

"Ben wasn't very fast, but he had an uncanny knack of being able to get away from defensive backs," said Ryan Hite. "I'd throw a ball to the flat and, after he made the catch, he could stand still and juke the defender without even moving, just kind of shift his body and go. He had great hands, too; he would catch everything."

Interestingly, Hite, who is currently the offensive coordinator at Gallaudet University, went on to Denison University, a Division III school, and won the starting quarterback job in his freshman year. But, after compiling more than 1,500 yards of total offense that season, he lost the starting job the following season and switched to wide receiver.

"I had never played as a receiver, and my father would tell you that I didn't have any of the skills to play the position, other than speed," said Hite, who caught 63 passes in his sophomore season and went on to earn all-conference honors and establish more than a few school records. "But maybe my dad was wrong."

During the summer before his senior year, Roethlisberger and some of his Trojan teammates attended a football camp on the campus of the University of Pittsburgh. Coach Hite intended to install a passing offense in order to take full advantage of Roethlisberger's passing ability, and he thought that the camp would provide an ideal opportunity to jump-start the process.

"It was Ben's real debut as a quarterback, and he tore it up," recalled Hite. "By the time we left the campus, we knew that it was going to be a good season for us."

One interested observer had been Terry Hoeppner, who was the head coach at Miami University, in Oxford, Ohio.

"I liked him, but I wasn't about to offer a scholarship to a kid before I saw him play a game," said Hoeppner, who passed away in 2007. "Ben certainly had a live arm. One NFL scout told me that he could hear the ball move through the air when Ben threw it. But, a strong arm and a seven-on-seven drill is one thing; you have to see what a quarterback can do in a game, when he has guys in his face. I didn't want to be the genius who offered a scholarship to a guy who never played quarterback."

In the first game of his senior season Roethlisberger showed what he could do with *guys in his face* by throwing six touchdown passes, which really was all the proof that Hoeppner needed.

Eventually, Duke also offered a scholarship, and Houston Rockets' forward Shane Battier, a former Blue Devils' hoop star, showed him around the campus. Ohio State also made an offer, but the coaching staff wouldn't commit to playing him at quarterback, and he was annoyed at the fact that the coaching staff couldn't pronounce his name. In the end, he decided to accept the offer from Hoeppner, despite the fact that Miami played in the Mid-American Conference, which lacked the cachet of major conferences, like the Big Ten, in which Ohio State plays.

"It came down to what felt right for me and where I thought I would be most comfortable," said Roethlisberger, whose tough style of play had earned him the nickname *Rotty*, a shortened form of Rottweiler. "I also talked to my family, and Miami just seemed to be the right fit for me."

Before he left Findlay, however, Roethlisberger became a record-smashing star, who set the Ohio state marks for passing yards (4,041) and touchdown passes (54), while leading the Trojans to a 10-2 season and into the second round of the state playoffs. Roethlisberger was named the Division 1 Offensive Player of the Year, and finished as the 1999 runner-up for Ohio's Mr. Football honors.

"I watch him do things now and it never shocks me," said Cliff Hite, who dropped out of coaching and teaching a few years ago and won a seat in the Ohio House of Representatives using the slogan *Hite is Right*. "I laugh when the announcer says, 'How'd he do that?' I saw him do it a hundred times when he played for Findlay."

2   BIG BEN

When coach Hoeppner visited the Roethlisberger home in December of 1999 to finalize the scholarship arrangement, he told his new recruit that he wanted him to emulate Chad Pennington, who was on his way to leading Marshall, which was the dominant team in the Mid-American Conference, to a perfect 13-0 record. Pennington had helped put the conference on the football map two years earlier when he and wide receiver Randy Moss set an NCAA record by combining for 24 touchdown passes, the most touchdowns ever thrown by one quarterback to one receiver in a single season. Moss went on to become a No. 1 pick of the Minnesota Vikings in the 1998 draft, and the New York Jets selected Pennington in the first round of the 2000 draft.

"I told Ben right away, 'I want you to be the next Chad Pennington of this league,' and Chad just happened to be on his way to New York because he was a finalist for the Heisman Trophy," recalled Hoeppner, speaking about the most highly-prized award in college football. "But I didn't make any guarantees. I told him that he would have to win the job."

In reality, Roethlisberger didn't have any chance to win the starting job when he arrived on campus in 2000, because the quarterback position was in the capable hands of senior Mike Bath. So, instead of wasting a year of eligibility, Roethlisberger was red-shirted, and he watched as Bath, who is now an assistant coach at Miami, finished out his final season with the RedHawks by establishing school-career records for passing yards, 6,524, and touchdowns thrown, 49.

Even after Bath had graduated, Roethlisberger found himself in a struggle for the starting job with Ryan Hawk, who was also starting his second year with Miami.

"Ben and Ryan made it a close battle all the way to the end of summer camp," said Hoeppner. "It was the kind of competition that gets a coach like me excited for the start of the season."

Winning the starting job was the good news. The bad news was that the RedHawks' first two games were on the road against a pair of powerful Big Ten teams, starting with Michigan, a perennial contender for national honors, and then the Iowa Hawkeyes.

"His first start is going to be in front of 100,000 people, none of whom are going to be rooting for us," said Hoeppner. "But, judging by what I know and have seen, he's a guy who seems to rise up and meet whatever athletic challenge he has to face."

Despite the coach's confidence, Michigan, which was ranked No. 10 in the nation, rolled over Miami, 31-13, as the first two touchdown passes of Roethlisberger's college career were more than offset by a trio of interceptions.

"It was great to play my first game, but I'd sure like to get those picks back," said Roethlisberger. "Everything happened so much faster than I thought it would, but you can't simulate that kind of intensity on the practice field."

Things went downhill the following week, as the Hawkeyes grounded the RedHawks 44-19, and the final score actually made the game look a lot closer than it actually was. The Hawkeyes were so dominant that Miami was shut out until the third quarter, and they didn't get on the scoreboard until Iowa had already scored all of its points and was freely substituting. Although Roethlisberger had decent stats, including another pair of touchdown tosses and an 80-yard touchdown run, all of it came in garbage time, when the outcome of the game had already been decided.

"That was ugly," acknowledged Roethlisberger, who was picked off twice and sacked five times, and didn't complete his first pass until the third quarter. "We're going to have to regroup and begin playing a lot better than we did today."

The RedHawks finally got to play their first home game of the season, against Cincinnati, and Roethlisberger gave the Miami fans something to cheer about when he connected on a 43-yard touchdown play with freshman wide receiver Michael Larkin on the game's opening drive. Roethlisberger went on to have an amazingly efficient game, as he completed 20 of his 25 pass attempts, threw for a second touchdown later in the game and ran for a third score, as the RedHawks gained their first win of the season, 21-14, over the Bearcats, their long-time arch-rival. His accomplishments were recognized by the conference coaches, who named him the MAC Offensive Player of the Week.

"I'm really proud of Ben," said Hoeppner. "I think you saw the real Ben Roethlisberger today."

The victory against Cincinnati was the start of a seven-game winning streak, with Roethlisberger acting as the ignition switch for Miami's high-octane offense.

After squeaking by Ball State, the RedHawks soared over Buffalo, 31-14, which made Miami the first MAC team to win six hundred games. Roethlisberger, who threw another pair of touchdown passes, was, again, named the MAC Offensive Player of the Week. Roethlisberger raised his game to an entirely new level the following week against Akron, however, when he threw for three touchdowns and set school records for passing yards, with 399, and total offense, with 485 yards. Roethlisberger capped his amazing day by throwing a 70-yard touchdown strike to Eddie Tillitz on the final play of the game, which rallied the RedHawks to a 30-27 win. That play cinched his third Offensive Player of the Week award and it also earned him a new nickname, *Big Ben.*

"It might have helped that he was thrown into the fire early on against Michigan and Iowa, because, really, the light turned on afterwards," said Shane Montgomery, who was Miami's offensive coordinator at the time and is now its head coach. "I don't know that I've ever seen a young quarterback have a better game or make a bigger play."

Although there was no final-play drama the following week, Roethlisberger again lit up the scoreboard in a big way by throwing five touchdown passes, which tied the RedHawk record, and rallied Miami to a 36-24 win over the Ohio University Bobcats.

"I'm not really into records," said Roethlisberger, who threw two of his TD passes in the decisive fourth quarter. "What's important is that we picked up another win and we're on a pretty good roll right now."

The RedHawks continued along their merry way with a win over Western Michigan, as Roethlisberger added two more touchdown passes to his growing total. They won their seventh straight game the following week, with a 24-21 triumph against Bowling Green, as Roethlisberger passed for another pair of scores, including an 81-yarder to Michael Larkin, and threw for 305 yards, which allowed him to break the MAC freshman mark for passing yards in a season.

"I know that Ben is a great deal more interested in the win than he is in the record, but it's still a wonderful accomplishment," said Hoeppner. "And, if he keeps playing like this, he's going to break a great many more records."

The seven-game winning streak put the RedHawks in position to capture the MAC East Division title, but the Thundering Herd from Marshall, who were also riding a seven-game win streak, came into Oxford and snatched away that dream with a 27-21 triumph. The victory vaulted the 8-1 Thundering Herd to their fifth consecutive division title, while Roethlisberger was held without a touchdown pass for the first time in his college career.

The RedHawks took flight for their next contest, flying across the Pacific Ocean to play their first-ever game against the University of Hawaii Warriors. Roethlisberger rebounded from the Marshall game in a big way, as he completed 40 of 53 passes for 452 yards, which were more than enough for him to eclipse the school's single-season record of 2,525 that had been set by Mike Bath in 1999. Big Ben also ran for one score and threw for three more, the last of which gave Miami a 51-49 lead with only a minute left in the game.

Unfortunately, that was just enough time for Hawaii to position itself for a game-winning field goal and escape with a 52-51 victory. Although their field goal kicker, Justin Ayat had supplied the winning points, the Warriors' real hero was quarterback Nick Rolovich, who racked up *seven* touchdown passes and threw for *500* yards in his once-in-a-lifetime performance.

"All losses hurt, but that was a heart-breaker," said Roethlisberger, who had set school records for completions, passing yards and all-purpose yards. "The flight here was long enough, but the return trip is going to seem that much longer."

The RedHawks ran into another red-hot quarterback in their season-ending, 24-20, loss at Kent State, although Joshua Cribbs, the Golden Flashes' quarterback, who ran for 151 yards and two touchdowns, did a lot more damage with his legs than he did with his arm. But they also ran into a bone-crunching defense, which held Miami to −1 yard rushing and held the high-scoring RedHawks' offense to a single touchdown.

"That defense smelled blood," said Hoeppner. "They were like sharks in a feeding frenzy."

The main attacker for Kent State was senior linebacker James Harrison, who made 12 tackles, including five behind the line of scrimmage, forced a fumble, and had four sacks, including two that slammed the door on Miami's last-ditch final drive. The sacks served as an exclamation point on the college career of Harrison, who is now Roethlisberger's teammate on the Pittsburgh Steelers.

"He made so many plays that they must have thought he had a twin," said Kent State coach Dan Pees, who had guided the Flashes to their first winning season since 1987. "He played like a man possessed."

The assessment by Pees didn't draw any arguments from Roethlisbeger, who was harried and battered throughout the game.

"I've never been hit harder or more often than I was today," said Roethlisberger, who was sacked five times and picked off twice, while throwing for 238 yards and one touchdown. "It's a good thing we don't have to practice for a while."

Although there was no denying the fact that the three-game losing streak was a disappointing way to close out their schedule, the RedHawks had still managed to finish with a 7-5 record, their eighth straight winning season. And, with Roethlisberger calling the signals, the future looked even brighter than the past.

Big Ben, who had set single-season school records for passing yards (3,105); completions (241); touchdowns (25); completion percentage (63.3) and total offense (3,294), had, without question, put together the best season ever for a RedHawk quarterback. In fact, Roethlisberger, who was selected as Miami's MVP and was also named to the Freshman All-America Team by the Football Writers Association of America, had crafted one of the best seasons ever by any first-year college quarterback.

"I thought that he would be good, but I had no idea that he would be *this* good, and I certainly couldn't have predicted that he would develop so quickly," said Hoeppner. "The fact that he was named to the All-America Team speaks for itself."

3   RUNNING IN PLACE

Roethlisberger's first season at the helm of the Miami offense had exceeded any reasonable expectations, including Hoeppner's, as the squad had posted the third-highest yardage total in school history. But the RedHawks' coach was expecting him to soar even higher in his second season.

"Ben's coming off a big year, and we hope he will build on that," said Hoeppner, right before the start of the 2002 season. "We asked him to do a lot as a freshman, and he handled it pretty well. But he has to continue to grow for us to improve as a team. It's true that we gained a lot of yards last season, but we also squandered a lot of opportunities to convert some of that yardage into points. We've challenged Ben to become more efficient, and now he needs to take those strides."

Roethlisberger realized that his development as a quarterback was still a work in progress, and he relished the opportunity to rise to the coach's challenge and take the next step in that process.

"In high school, I played quarterback for only the one year, so there are still some aspects of the game that I need to improve in," he acknowledged. "In fact, I need to improve across the board. I've worked really hard during the off-season to do just that, and the coaching staff has worked just as hard to help me smooth out the rough edges. Now, it's on me to step it up, and to try to help the team compete for a championship."

With thirteen starters returning from the 2001 team, both the coach and the quarterback had reason to approach the upcoming season with optimism. Unfortunately, they would be disappointed at the way the season unfolded and, especially, at the way it ended.

The RedHawks started off on the right foot by beating North Carolina in the season-opener, 27-21. Roethlisberger, who threw for 204 yards and a touchdown, had a solid game, despite a torrential rain that helped cause *nine* turnovers by the Tar Heels, including six by their quarterback. Roethlisberger also punted twice, including a 59-yard boomer, which was the longest punt by a Miami player in more than a year.

Miami hosted Iowa the following week, and they hung tough with a Hawkeye team that would go on to play in the Orange Bowl after sharing the Big Ten title with Ohio State. But despite a big day by Roethlisberger, who totaled 343 passing-yards and two TD tosses, the RedHawks had their wings clipped, 29-24.

"He's a tremendous football player and very tough to defend against," said Iowa coach Kirk Ferentz. "I'm just glad that we were able to run out the clock at the end of the fourth quarter and keep him off the field. I didn't want the ball in his hands again."

The RedHawks flew south to play Louisiana State University, another nationally ranked team, and the Tigers of LSU lived up to their nickname by mauling Miami, 33-7.

Although the RedHawks were only three games into their new season, there were already indications that the confidence they had felt before their first game might have been misplaced. The game marked a statistical low point in the four-year tenure of Hoeppner, who had never before fielded a Miami team that had scored so few points or lost by so many. And with their 1-2 record, the RedHawks had lost five of their past six games dating back to the previous season. This was the roughest patch of road that a Miami team had traveled since 1993.

The RedHawks rebounded the following week, however, with a 27-20 win at home over Kent State, providing a successful launch to the Mid-American Conference portion of their schedule. Although Roethlisberger had a choppy game, RedHawks' running back Luke Clemens picked up the offensive slack by romping for 171 yards and a pair of touchdowns.

"I was a little out of sync today," admitted Roethlisberger, who was held under 200 yards passing for the second consecutive game. "However, our running game was dominant today, and Luke did a great job. Sometimes, when the passing attack isn't working, you have to run the ball. I think we did a great job of adjusting today."

The RedHawks' offense finally managed to get itself in gear the following week, and Miami brought down Akron, 48-31. Luke Clemens once again supplied a spark by rumbling for 135 yards and a trio of touchdowns, while Roethlisberger supplied a steady hand and contributed 240 passing yards and a pair of touchdown tosses, including a 50-yard strike to wide receiver Korey Kirkpatrick.

"I like the way we bounced back after they had us down 14-0," said Hoeppner. "Although the offense didn't really start to click until the second half, once they got it going, they just kept on rolling."

The RedHawks stretched their modest winning streak to three games with a 31-26 triumph over Cincinnati, giving them back-to-back wins over the Bearcats for the first time since 1991-1992. Clemens topped the 100-yard mark for the third consecutive time and added another pair of scores to his rapidly increasing total, while Roethlisberger complemented the running game by completing 27 of 37 passing attempts, including a single touchdown toss. The score that put Miami in the lead for good, however, was produced by back-up quarterback Josh Betts, who converted a fake field goal into a 13-yard TD pass to tight end Tyler Vogel.

"We had to grind all day and pull some tricks out of the bag," said Roethlisberger. "But that's why the coaches put them in the playbook."

Big Ben finally showed up for the first time in the 2002 season the following week, as Roethlisberger racked up a school-record 525 passing yards, threw for four scores, ran for another, and broke his own MAC mark for completions by connecting on 41 of 61 attempts against Northern Illinois University. Unfortunately for him and the RedHawks, that explosive output was more than matched by Huskies' running back Michael *The Burner* Turner, who ran for 222 yards and tallied five touchdowns, as NIU rallied for 34 *fourth-quarter* points and pulled out a 48-41 victory.

Despite the loss and despite having three of his passes picked, Roethlisberger's otherwise astonishing performance earned his first East Division Offensive Player of the Week award for the 2002 season.

"The one number that stands out for me is the three interceptions that I threw," said Roethlisberger, who took no joy in the big numbers that he had posted. "The bottom line is we lost the game."

Coach Hoeppner, meanwhile, was shocked by the inability of his defense to fend off the Huskies' unrelenting fourth-quarter charge, and took responsibility for the staff's failure to devise a scheme to slow the offensive onslaught.

"I'm shocked that they could score that many points in a 15-minute span," he said. "I know that it was a special and incredible effort on their part, but we have to take a hard look at our performance, starting with the coaching staff. That being said, we're disappointed but we're not discouraged. We're not going to give up."

The RedHawks responded to that deflating loss with a 49-0 beating of a hapless Buffalo team, which had lost its previous game by a 66-19 score. Clemens set the tone by scoring Miami's first two touchdowns, while Roethlisberger, who played less than three quarters, contributed 228 yards and three touchdown passes, including a pair to wide receiver Jason Branch.

Miami rode their momentum to a 27-13 win over Toledo, ending the Rockets' 17-game home winning streak. Roethlisberger had an efficient game at quarterback, passing for 299 yards, without an interception, and leading the RedHawks on five scoring drives. He was also given the opportunity to punt three times, and in each instance he pinned down the Rockets inside their own 10-yard line. That showing earned him the MAC East Division Special Teams Player of the Week award.

"Although Ben's not our regular punter, he's done an amazing job every time we've called on him," said Hoeppner. "When you can pin a team back inside its own 10-yard line, it's a big help to the defense, of course. But lots of times, it also helps the offense, because if the other team can't move the ball and is forced to punt it back to us, we're likely to wind up with very good field position."

Miami won its third-straight game the following week, with a 38-20 win over Ohio, as Clemens scored twice on the ground and Roethlisberger struck through the air with a pair of touchdown passes to Michael Larkin.

"Our offense is really talented, both running and throwing the ball," said Roethlisberger. "Our line didn't give up any sacks, our running backs ran hard, and our wide receivers did their thing. When our offense clicks, we're pretty good."

The win had upped Miami's overall record to 7-3, and 5-1 in the MAC conference, which gave them a half-game lead in the East Division over their next opponent, Marshall University. The RedHawks had lost their four most recent match-ups with Marshall, a school they had started playing against in 1905, and they fell behind in this one, too, as first-time starting quarterback Stan Hill, who was subbing for the injured Byron Leftwich, sparked the Thundering Herd to a 17-3 lead. Rather than allowing the score or the frenzied Marshall fans to intimidate them, the RedHawks rallied to tie the game on a pair of second-quarter scoring strikes by Roethlisberger.

The Herd thundered into the lead again in the third quarter, however, when Hill connected on his third and fourth touchdown passes of the game, both of which were caught by wide receiver Darius Watts, giving him three in the game. The RedHawks bounced right back, however, as Roethlisberger led them on three scoring drives, the last of which gave Miami a 34-29 lead with 6:33 left to play.

After a Marshall drive was halted at the Miami 27-yard line, Miami got the ball back with 2:38 left, only needing a first down or two to run out the clock. But the RedHawks lost a couple of yards on two running plays, and then Roethlisberger was sacked on third down, which forced Miami to punt the ball back to Marshall.

With the ball on their own 43-yard line, and 1:39 to play, Hill drove the Herd down the field, helped by two pass interference calls against Miami. Then, with the ball perched on the Miami 1-yard line and ten ticks left on the clock, Hill toted the ball around left end and into the end zone to give Marshall a 36-34 win.

Roethlisberger, who had three TD tosses and a costly interception that set up Marshall's first touchdown, finished the game as Miami's all-time completions leader, with 489, and he also rose into second place on the school's list for career touchdown passes, with 46. But those numbers seemed meaningless compared to the ones posted on the scoreboard.

"I suppose they'll mean something to me at some future point," said Roethlisberger. "But right now, I just feel empty."

The RedHawks' season came to a dreary and almost anti-climatic end the following week with a 48-31 loss to the University of Central Florida, which dropped their record to 7-5, exactly the same as they had posted the year before.

"We crumbled today," said Hoeppner, his clipped tones highlighting his harsh words. "We were fragile. When we lost the momentum, we couldn't get it back. Their quarterback played a great game. We couldn't come up with the key play."

Roethlisberger, who broke his own previous single-season school record by passing for 3,238 yards, became the first quarterback in Miami history to top 3,000 yards in consecutive seasons. He passed with great accuracy, threw twice as many touchdowns as interceptions, repeated as the team's MVP, and was also named to the MAC Second Team on a vote by the conference's head coaches.

Despite all those accomplishments and awards, however,

the season had ended disappointingly, much like the previous season. In fact, it seemed as though Roethlisberger and the RedHawks hadn't really moved forward, but had merely run in place.

4   GOING OUT IN STYLE

Coach Hoeppner looked forward to the 2003 season with great expectations of winning the conference championship and earning an invitation to a post-season bowl game. His high hopes were riding on what he considered to be an excellent mix of new players and returning lettermen, and an offense centered on his junior quarterback.

"These guys are on a mission, and they think they're ready to compete against anyone," said Hoeppner, who placed the main burden of meeting the team's high expectations on Roethlisberger's shoulders. "If you look at this conference, it seems that the team with the best quarterback wins it. Hopefully, that will give us an advantage this year. I've seen a lot of growth and maturity in Ben, and I think he's doing a very good job of handling his responsibilities as a team leader and dealing with all the media attention he's been receiving. That kind of stuff can either distract you or motivate you, and Ben has maintained his focus on what's important."

The attention lavished on Roethlisberger included an *ESPN The Magazine* article that ranked him as the 23rd best player in college football. The only quarterbacks ranked ahead of him were North Carolina State's Philip Rivers, at No. 18, and Missouri's Brad Smith, at 20.

"The prototype can make all the throws, even run the option, and now he has a deep threat in Martin Nance," said the story's writer, Bruce Feldman.

"We want to go undefeated and win the MAC this year,"

said Roethlisberger, in defiance of a schedule that had them going on the road against a trio of tough opponents in their first three games. "You have to set your sights as high as you can, and those are our two big ones."

Despite that show of confidence, after a 21-3 season-opening loss to Iowa, the first of the two major goals was DOA, and the major reason for the defeat was the poor play of Roethlisberger, who suffered five sacks and threw four interceptions, a career high.

"Obviously, that's not the way I planned to start the season," said Roethlisberger. "But I still believe in the mission that we dedicated ourselves to, and I think that we'll bounce back in our next game."

He proved to be as good a prophet as he is a quarterback, as the RedHawks routed Northwestern, 44-14. Big Ben, who threw for 353 yards and no interceptions, sparked the onslaught with three scoring passes, including a 61-yarder to Martin Nance. The strike to Nance, the 50th touchdown pass of his career, made him the school's career-leader in passing touchdowns, and it also moved him to the top of the school's total yardage list, with 7,090.

That demonstration of virtuosity earned Roethlisberger the East Division Offensive Player of the Week award, and it also marked the start of a season-long display of offensive fireworks that would see records set almost every time he threw a pass.

The RedHawks completed their three-game road trip by clobbering Colorado State, 41-21, as Roethlisberger connected for another pair of scores and racked up 330 yards through the air, to become the only player in school history to pass for 7,000 yards.

Miami came home to play in front of a sold-out Yager

Stadium, and they rewarded that support by beating Cincinnati, 42-37, their third straight capture of the Victory Bell trophy that goes to the winner of this long-time annual rivalry. Roethlisberger delighted the crowd by throwing for two scores and 377 yards, becoming the first Miami quarterback with three straight 300-yard games.

If Miami fans felt a sense of déjà vu the following week, it was understandable, because the RedHawks downed Akron 45-20, and Roethlisberger, who was again named East Division Offensive Player of the Week, ripped the Zips' defense for 369 yards and another pair of touchdown passes.

"In the beginning of the season I said that I thought we had the best quarterback in the conference," said Hoeppner. "I think Ben is, without a doubt, living up to that potential."

The RedHawks hosted Buffalo the following week and they battered their defenseless guests, 59-3. Roethlisberger threw for three first-half scores, two of which went to Michael Larkin, including a 30-yarder that opened the floodgates. It was the 17th time that the two juniors had connected on a scoring play for Miami, the most of any duo in school history. Freshman wide receiver Ryne Robinson also had a big first quarter, as he took consecutive punts to the house, the first one covering 86 yards and the next one going for 76 yards. In all, Robinson totaled a MAC-record 239 yards on six punt returns.

The 59 points were the most scored by Miami since Hoeppner had taken over as the head coach, and the 45 that they put on the scoreboard in the first two quarters broke the school record of 35 first-half points that had been set in 2000.

"Success breeds success," said Hoeppner, who had watched his team score 40-plus points for the fourth consecutive game, another RedHawks' record. "The guys are feeling good about themselves and cutting loose and making plays. I like the way we're playing on both sides of the line of scrimmage and the special teams are also playing extremely well. We're playing fast; we're attacking; we're taking it to the other teams."

The RedHawks continued to live up to their predatory nickname the following week by devouring the Cardinals from Ball State, 49-3, as Roethlisberger burned the MAC's top-ranked pass defense for a pair of touchdown strikes.

"Ben has a great arm and he's obviously very blessed athletically, but I think his decision-making is also outstanding," said the Cardinals' head coach, Brady Hoke. "You can tell that he's the leader of that team."

The six-game winning streak earned Miami a No. 23 ranking in the initial Bowl Championship Series Poll of the 2002 season, the first time since the BCS Poll was started in 1998 that the RedHawks had been ranked in the top 25. They were joined in the ranking by two other MAC teams: Northern Illinois, who claimed the 10th spot, and Bowling Green, who was right behind Miami, at 24.

"Our team is very deserving of this distinction because a great deal of hard work by each member of the team has gone into getting us to this point," said Hoeppner. "My hope is to build on this and, hopefully, continue to play at the same high level."

After meeting little resistance in their three previous contests, The RedHawks found themselves in a back-and-forth battle against Kent State the following week that quickly developed into a game of *can-you-top-this* between

Roethlisberger and the Golden Flashes' quarterback, Joshua Cribbs.

After getting off to a bad start by throwing his first interception in 114 pass attempts, Roethlisberger righted the ship by leading Miami on four first-half scoring drives, and the RedHawks went into the locker room with a 24-14 lead. But Cribbs, who had already thrown for one first-half touchdown and run for another, ran the ball in for a second score in the third quarter, and then put Kent State in the lead, 27-24, with a 21-yard touchdown pass at the start of the fourth quarter.

Although he hadn't played in a meaningful fourth quarter the entire season, Roethlisberger responded to the challenge by leading Miami on two successive scoring drives, capping both of them with touchdown strikes to Nance, their second and third scoring collaborations of the day. A field goal by Kent State narrowed the lead with just under three minutes to play, but it was too little, too late, and the RedHawks prevailed, 38-30.

The following week, Miami played host to Bowling Green, in the first ever nationally-televised game at Yager Stadium. The match-up was a conference showdown between a pair of 7-1 teams, with the Falcons ranked first in the MAC in both offense and defense, and the RedHawks right behind them in second place in each of the categories.

Roethlisberger got off to a shaky start by losing a fumble and throwing an interception, but then he steadied down and guided Miami to 23 second-half points and a surprisingly easy 33-10 win.

Although he failed to throw a touchdown pass, he did run for one score and he also set up another one with a play-action fake that allowed Nance to get behind a safety and snare a 49-yard pass at the Bowling Green 5-yard line.

"Tonight's win was a tribute to our team," said Hoeppner. "It was a tough game and we had to overcome a sloppy first half, but we'll remember the second half for a long time."

The RedHawks' next game was against Marshall, in the second televised game from Yager Stadium, and only the third night game in the stadium's history. Although the temperature was mild at kick-off, the wind, which was gusting at more than thirty miles an hour, caused the goal posts to sway and the flag poles to bend.

"I was trying to not get blown away," said Roethlisberger, who managed to send his throws spiraling through the swirling wind for 282 yards and a pair of touchdowns. "I told the receivers that the passes might not be pretty, but that I would get them there."

Roethlisberger, who started the scoring with a 14-yard touchdown pass on the game's first possession also ended it with a 10-yard fourth-quarter dart, as the RedHawks triumphed over their recent nemesis, 45-6, and clinched the East Division title.

Roethlisberger was named the Player of the Week for the third time in the 2002 season, and the eighth time in his three years in Oxford.

"Ben's a great quarterback, but I've seen enough of him," said Bob Pruett, Marshall's head coach. "I hope he decides to skip his last year and enter the NFL draft. If he does, he should definitely be a first-round pick."

Roethlisberger and the RedHawks continued on their roll the following week, as the quarterback passed for 294 yards and four scores in three quarters of play, and led Miami past Ohio University, 49-31. By the end of the game, the team had set school records for yards and points in a season, while extending their winning streak to 10 games. After the game, the team accepted an invitation to play in the GMAC Bowl.

"Our aim at the beginning of the year was to play 14 games, and we've achieved that goal now," said Hoeppner. "But first we have a couple of pieces of unfinished business to take care of."

The RedHawks took care of the first piece of business by pounding the University of Central Florida, 56-21, to finish the regular season with a perfect 8-0 mark in MAC play. Their 12 wins overall eclipsed the team record of 11, which had been reached twice, and the 56 points gave Miami a total of 504 points in 12 games, breaking the MAC record of 495 that had been set by Toledo over 14 games a year earlier.

Roethlisberger, meanwhile, who continued to set new standards, was an almost-perfect 24-of-29, while throwing for 327 yards and five touchdowns, before leaving the game early in the third quarter. The touchdown passes upped his total to 29, which broke his own school single-season record; and he also became the first player in Miami history and only the 30th in Division I-A to reach 10,000 yards of total offense in a career.

It was also a record-setting day for two of his receivers: Michael Larkin, who had caught two touchdown passes, which upped his career total to 21, a new school record; and Martin Nance, who had over 100 yards receiving for the sixth time, a single-season school record.

"Ben has made a quantum leap forward this season in regard to his comfort level and, therefore, his ability to command the offense," said Hoeppner. "Byron Leftwich told me that the game had slowed done for him in his third year, and that's exactly what's happened with Ben."

For the MAC Championship game, Miami had to travel to Bowling Green in a rematch against the West Division winners, who had finished their regular season with a 10-2 mark. The Falcons managed to stick close to the RedHawks in the first half, despite a trio of touchdown passes from Roethlisberger, and they went into their locker room trailing by only four points, 21-17. But Roethlisberger led Miami to 28 second-half points, including a 55-yard touchdown pass to Cal Murray, and the RedHawks cruised to a 49-27 win and their first MAC Championship since 1986.

In addition to his four touchdown passes, Roethlisberger threw for 440 yards, breaking the MAC Championship game mark of 421 that had been set by Byron Leftwich in 2001.

"All I had to do was put it out there, and they made the plays," said Roethlisberger, who was named the MAC Offensive Player of the Year. "And I can't say enough about the offensive line. Look, my jersey is still white."

Although he spoke as if he had just gone along for the ride, the two coaches knew otherwise.

"I can't wait to play them after he's gone," said Gregg Brandon, the Bowling Green coach. "We had no answer for him. When we did manage to generate some pressure, he eluded it and still found his receivers, and they ran by us all day."

"It's only people who see him for the first time who are surprised," said Hoeppner, who was named the MAC Coach of the Year. "The rest of us have almost grown accustomed to his amazing skill and productivity."

The RedHawks continued to ride Roethlisberger's right arm in the GMAC Bowl, and he delivered the goods by passing for 376 yards and four more touchdowns, as Miami romped over Louisville, 49-28, and stretched their longest-in-the-nation winning streak to 13.

"He made some plays that made those of you who haven't seen him play in person go, 'How can he *do* that? How can he keep escaping like that and hitting guys' hands with the ball?'" said Hoeppner. "I think he's the finest college quarterback in the country."

Roethlisberger, who was named the GMAC Bowl MVP, finished his amazing highlight reel of a season with the MAC single-season records for completions, passing yards, and total offense, and joined Byron Leftwich and Chad Pennington as the MAC quarterbacks to total 11,000 yards in their careers.

Afterwards, surrounded by his family, coach Hoeppner and some of his closest teammates, Roethlisberger, who was named a Third-Team All-American by the Associated Press, announced his intention to forego his last season of eligibility and enter the 2004 NFL draft.

"The unbelievable team success this season has fulfilled so many of my collegiate football goals," said Roethlisberger, who led the RedHawks to their first post-season win in 28 years, and helped them to finish the season as the 10th ranked team in the nation. "I'll always be grateful for the wonderful experiences I've had here in the past four years, but now I feel the time is right to embark on the next challenge."

5   BLACK AND GOLD

After Roethlisberger decided to enter the draft, he hired Leigh Steinberg, a well-respected agent, to represent him in future negotiations. Steinberg is the only sports agent who insists that every contract he negotiates for his players include clauses that require the athlete to make substantial charitable donations.

"Leigh has been a legend in the business for many years, and I wanted to be with the best," explained Roethlisberger. "His firm places an emphasis on doing work in the community and being a role model, which are critical issues for me."

Steinberg has a long history of representing top-flight athletes, including Warren Moon, Steve Young and Troy Aikman, a trio of Hall of Fame quarterbacks, and Matt Leinart, the Arizona Cardinals' young signal-caller. In Steinberg's eyes, Roethlisberger had the potential to become an elite NFL quarterback

"Ben is a gifted, franchise-type quarterback, with the tools to be picked at the top of the draft," said Steinberg, who has represented the No. 1 overall pick a record eight times. "He possesses a rare combination of incredible arm strength, athleticism and leadership qualities."

Most NFL talent evaluators largely agreed with the agent's assessment, including Mike Martz, who had helped Kurt Warner become an NFL MVP and an All-Pro quarterback with the St. Louis Rams when Martz was the team's head coach.

"Everything you've read about him is accurate," said Martz, who led the Rams and their explosive offense to an NFL title in Super Bowl XXXIV. "He has a big arm, he moves well in the pocket and he can make some yards when he's flushed out. He reads defenses well, doesn't get rattled when the pressure comes, and he was a great teammate. It's all good."

The only real question seemed to be whether or not Roethlisberger would make a better pro football player than the other two highly-rated quarterbacks available in the draft, namely Philip Rivers and Eli Manning, the younger brother of Peyton Manning, the quarterback for the Indianapolis Colts.

As the teams prodded and poked the players, and watched thousands of hours of tape, fans all around the country lit up the lines of sports call-in shows and internet chat rooms, debating the relative merits of the three quarterbacks. Sportswriters and television talking heads weighed in with their views, too. Every one, it seemed, had an opinion, but no one had an answer, not even the players themselves.

"This thing is like a roller coaster," said Roethlisberger, about the constantly changing rumors of how the draft would play out. "It's a game. No one really knows what the teams are going to do. It's certainly not like college, where I got to choose where I wanted to go."

As the first day of the April draft drew closer, the word on the grapevine was that Eli Manning would be the first of the three quarterbacks selected, an opinion that Roethlisberger seemed to second.

"He's got everything, including the name," said Roethlisberger, alluding not only to Peyton, but to their father, Archie, a former Pro Bowl quarterback for the

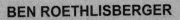

New Orleans Saints. "Hands down, Eli Manning is a great quarterback. He is, right now, the No. 1 pick in the draft according to a lot of people. He deserves it. I just love watching him play."

In fact, Manning was selected first, by the San Diego Chargers, and Rivers went to the New York Giants three picks later, and then the teams turned around and exchanged the two players as part of a larger trade, because Manning refused to play for the Chargers.

Cleveland had the sixth pick, and the fans in Findlay were hoping that the Browns would keep Roethlisberger in Ohio, but the team opted, instead, to take Kellen Winslow, Jr., a tight end who is the son of a Hall of Fame tight end.

"The fans back in Findlay took that really hard," said Jerry Snodgrass, Roethlisberger's former basketball coach. "And now, to see what he's doing in Pittsburgh? It's just driving Browns fans nuts."

While the draft was unfolding at Madison Square Garden, Roethlisberger, dressed in a black suit and gold tie, was sitting in a backstage room with his family, wondering, but not anxiously, when his name would be called.

"I remember looking across at Ben as teams passed him by, and he was very calm," recalled Ken Roethlisberger. "I think he felt that wherever he went, he would make it work out."

The Pittsburgh Steelers, who had the 11th pick, ended the suspense by using it on Roethlisberger. Although the team's front office had preferred Rivers and Manning, head coach Bill Cowher, was pleased with the selection.

"We don't have a high pick very often, so, when we had the opportunity to take a good, young quarterback who has tremendous upside, we grabbed him," said Cowher, in explaining why the Steelers hadn't used their selection to fill more pressing needs. "It was too golden an opportunity to pass up."

Roethlisberger, who was, coincidentally, already dressed in the Steelers' black and gold colors, also spoke about his potential.

"I've only really played quarterback for four years," he noted. "A lot of other players, like Manning and Rivers, have been at the position their entire lives, and some of them get to a certain point where they can't get much better. I'm just getting started. I think I still have a lot more room to develop and, once I get on the field, I have a great will to win."

Ken Roethlisberger heard the fire in his son's voice and saw the look in his eyes and knew exactly what he was thinking.

"I knew his attitude was, 'I'll show them what I can do and make those other teams sorry that they didn't pick me,'" he recalled.

"Ben's a special guy," said Hoeppner. "The people of Pittsburgh will love him."

6 ROOKIE

Roethlisberger had left college as one of the top quarterbacks in the nation, and he had signed a contract with the Steelers that turned him into an instant millionaire. He had also had the opportunity to meet most of his new teammates in a minicamp that Pittsburgh had organized in the spring. But while he was driving to the Steelers' summer training camp in Latrobe, Pennsylvania, he was feeling as anxious as the new boy in town on his way to his first day of fifth grade.

"I didn't know what to expect," said Roethlisberger, who, as a rookie, was back in the position of having to prove himself all over again. "I just wanted to learn the offense, try to learn to be a backup, and do whatever it was the coach was going to ask me to do. Mostly, I was trying to not get lost."

The nervousness that he was feeling stayed with him until after he had thrown his first pass, an overthrown spiral to Plaxico Burress, the team's 6-5 wide receiver, in a 7-on-7 passing drill. On his second attempt, Roethlisberger hit Burress between the numbers, and felt a weight lift off his shoulders.

"I overthrew him on the first one because I was so amped up, but I came back and got him with the next one," recalled Roethlisberger. "The butterflies were gone and it just felt good to be back on a football field."

The Steelers had drafted Roethlisberger because they

thought that he could, eventually, turn into a top-flight pro quarterback.

"The kid's potential is unlimited," said Kevin Colbert, Pittsburgh's director of football operations. "He hasn't reached his peak yet, but we're excited to know that when he does, he'll be a Steeler."

The short-term plan, however, was for Roethlisberger to spend the 2004 season on the bench, behind the veteran starter, Tommy Maddox, and his understudy, Charlie Batch. In essence, Pittsburgh planned to sideline Roethlisberger during his rookie season, much the way Miami had red-shirted him during his first season with the RedHawks.

"It's a good situation for him to be in," said coach Cowher. "With the veterans in front of him, he can watch and learn, and not have the pressure of trying to carry the team."

It didn't take long for the Steelers' plan to become inoperative, however, because Batch was forced to sit out the season on the injured reserve. Then Maddox, who had guided Pittsburgh to an opening game win against the Raiders, was knocked out of their second one early in the third quarter with an injury to his right elbow.

By the time Roethlisberger strapped on his helmet and ran on to the field, the Baltimore Ravens had already established a 20-0 lead. And the picture didn't get any brighter for Pittsburgh when they watched the rookie throw an interception on his second NFL pass.

Roethlisberger recovered quickly, however, and threw his first pair of NFL touchdown passes—the first one going to Antwaan Randle El, and the next one to Hines Ward—which narrowed the Steelers' deficit to 23-13. But any dreams of a dramatic debut were shattered on their following offensive series, when Ravens' cornerback Chris McCalister picked off a Roethlisberger pass and returned it for a game-clinching touchdown.

"They say I got my feet wet," said Roethlisberger, who finished the game with 176 passing yards on 12-of-20 attempts. "I think I got both of my legs wet."

Seeing their starting quarterback sidelined so early in the season was dismaying for the Pittsburgh players, who had spent the previous month enduring two-a-day practices, with the hot summer sun beating down on them. They had grunted through those grueling workouts for only one purpose, to make a run at the playoffs, and now it seemed that all their work might have been wasted.

"I wasn't happy," said the Steelers' All-Pro guard, Alan Faneca, who was speaking thoughts shared by most, if not all, of his teammates. "I didn't want our success to be in the hands of some young kid who was just out of college."

Faneca's worst fears seemed to be confirmed the following week when the Steelers went on the road and a Miami Dolphins' defender picked off Roethlisberger's first pass of the game.

"I was just shaking my head, looking at Hines like, 'I don't want to go this route,'" said Plaxico Burress.

"I was like, 'Uh, oh,'" said Jerome Bettis, a veteran running back and a team leader. "I could see the season slipping away almost before it had begun."

Roethlisberger kept his composure, however, despite playing through a hurricane-induced rainstorm that beat down on Pro Player Stadium, and led the visitors to a 13-3 win in his first NFL start.

"It was muddy and it was wet, but it was a lot of fun," said Roethlisberger, who had accounted for the game's only touchdown with a short fourth-quarter pass to Ward. "Playing in a hurricane and against that type of defense was a challenge for us, but we came out and did some good things."

Roethlisberger's performance earned him his first Pepsi NFL Rookie of the Week award, as well as the praise of his teammates and the Steelers' coaching staff.

"He never lost his composure, and just bounced right back after the interception," said Cowher. "He made some good decisions, and he was able to keep his footing, elude the rush and make some plays. He played well."

Roethlisberger also earned plaudits the following week when he led the Steelers on a long fourth-quarter scoring drive, which erased a Cincinnati Bengals' lead and paved the way for another Pittsburgh win, this time in front of their hometown fans at Heinz Field.

"He's still a rookie and he still makes mistakes," said Ward. "Overall, he's making more good plays than bad ones, and he's only going to get better as he becomes more comfortable with the offense."

The next opponent to come onto Heinz Field and challenge the Steelers was the Browns who, along with the Bengals and the Ravens, are Pittsburgh's rivals in the AFC North division. But the Steelers passed the test with a 34-23 win, as running back Duce Staley ran for 100 yards and Roethlisberger threw a 37-yard touchdown pass to Burress, and also scored his first NFL touchdown by diving into the end zone after a 6-yard scramble.

"He made some throws," said Cleveland defensive end Orpheus Roye. "You couldn't tell he was a rookie, because he played like a veteran."

The Steelers were scheduled to play in Dallas the following

week, but, before they arrived in the *Big D*, the Cowboys' coach, Bill Parcells, weighed in with his assessment of Roethlisberger and compared him to former Dolphins' great Dan Marino, who set the rookie record for passer rating and completion percentage, and has always been considered the Gold Standard when it comes to rookie quarterbacks.

"He is the best quarterback prospect I have seen in the past 10 or 15 years," declared Parcells. "Sure, he's going to have his growing pains, but he's in an ideal situation, because they have good balance on offense, and a defense that will usually keep them in any game. But I'm telling you, the only rookie quarterback who ever played like this kid is Dan Marino."

Although Roethlisberger appreciated the comments, he didn't allow them to swell his head.

"It's quite a compliment coming from someone who is so well respected in the community," said Roethlisberger. "But I've only started three games. It's a little too early to be comparing me to a Hall of Famer. If I can be half as good as Marino, I'll be very happy."

No one on the Steelers was feeling very good when they found themselves trailing the Cowboys, 20-10, in the fourth quarter. Even after Roethlisberger had led Pittsburgh on a long scoring drive, which he capped with a short touchdown toss, the Cowboys were still in position to run out the clock and win the game. But their veteran quarterback, Vinny Testaverde, fumbled the ball and the Steelers recovered it at the Dallas 24-yard line with 2:20 left on the clock. Instead of playing it safe by running time off the clock and then kicking a field goal to force overtime, Cowher put the ball and the game in his rookie's hands.

Roethlisberger responded by completing two passes,

first one to the left side and then another to the right side, which moved the ball to the Dallas seven. Bettis finished off the short drive by banging the ball into the end zone, and Pittsburgh left Dallas with a last-minute 24-20 win, which boosted their record to 5-1 and set the tone for the remainder of their season.

"That win may have been a turning point for us," said Cowher. "I think from there we just did whatever we had to do each week, and then looked ahead to the next challenge. That was the mindset that we developed."

Pittsburgh returned home to face the red-hot New England Patriots, who arrived at Heinz Field on Halloween day with an 18-game regular-season winning streak, 21 overall, including post-season play, both of which were NFL records. But the Steelers cooled them off and ended their streak, as Roethlisberger delivered the treats for Pittsburgh with two early touchdown passes to Burress and treated the Black and Gold to a 34-20 victory.

"That was a big win for us," said Roethlisberger, who was named the NFL Rookie of the Month for October. "It shows that we have the ability to play against anyone."

The Philadelphia Eagles and their 7-0 record followed the Patriots into Heinz Field and Roethlisberger, again, responded to the challenge by firing two first-half touchdown passes and leading the Steelers to a 27-3 triumph over their cross-state rivals. It was the first time that an NFL team had beaten undefeated teams back-to-back so late in the season.

"I try not to get overwhelmed," said Roethlisberger, when he was asked about how exciting it was to topple two undefeated teams, while outplaying the Patriots' Tom Brady and the Eagles' Donovan McNabb, two of the league's top quarterbacks. "I try to stay calm and level-headed."

Interestingly, Roethlisberger doesn't seem to have any trouble handling pressure when 80,000 screaming fans are generating ear-piercing levels of noise and 280-pound defensive ends are trying to drill their helmets through his rib cage. But he does get nervous when he plays in a pro-am golf match in front of a few thousand quiet fans.

"Too many people, and too much pressure," he explains. "I'm not good in front of people."

The Steelers went to 8-1 with a road win over the Browns, as Roethlisberger became the first rookie quarterback to win his first seven starts, and gave the Cleveland fans an up-close and personal look at the player that their team had passed over in the draft. Then, the Steelers traveled to Cincinnati, where they just barely escaped with a win, 19-14, as the Bengals battered Roethlisberger and sacked him seven times.

"I guess all of you were waiting for Ben to have a sub-par game, and I guess this was it," said Cowher, to the assembled reporters afterwards. "It was the first time I've seen him have a little bit of adversity. But he fought through it, didn't lose his composure or his confidence, and then came back and threw the winning touchdown pass. I think he grew a lot today."

The Steelers had another close call the following week in Washington, as Roethlisberger struggled, again, but the bruising running of Bettis, who wasn't nicknamed *The Bus* for nothing, bailed them out.

"I try to do the best I can, but I always miss something," said Roethlisberger, who was sacked four more times and completed only nine of his 20 pass attempts. "On some plays, I couldn't find the receivers that were open and, other times, I couldn't deliver the ball. But there's a game-to-game learning process that takes place, so hopefully, things will start to get better again."

He got back on track early in the game the following week in Jacksonville, when he stung the Jaguars for touchdown passes on the Steelers' first two possessions. But the Jacksonville defense tightened its grip and kept the Steelers off the scoreboard, while Byron Leftwich, their second-year quarterback, rallied the Jaguars into a 16-14 lead with 1:55 left to play.

The Steelers, without any timeouts left to stop the clock, were forced into their hurry-up offense, with Roethlisberger calling the plays from a shotgun formation.

"I told the guys. 'Let's complete a couple of passes, get the ball down the field and give Jeff a chance to win the game for us,'" said Roethlisberger, who then went on to move the Steelers down the field and into position for Jeff Reed to kick his game-winning 37-yard field goal.

"I want the ball in my hands in that situation," said Roethlisberger, who finished the game with a near-perfect 158.0 quarterback rating, and set an NFL record for victories by a rookie with his 10th win. "I want to control the outcome of the game."

Although the Pittsburgh players had watched admiringly as their rookie quarterback played beyond their wildest expectations, this latest performance raised the level of respect they felt for him.

"They came with all-out blitzes, and Ben just sat in the pocket and delivered the ball," said Antwaan Randle El. "We do the two-minute drill in practice, of course, but it doesn't mean anything until you have to deliver the throws in a big game, and he did that today."

Even Alan Faneca, who had been so distraught when Roethlisberger became the starter, was ready to tip his hat.

"The legend grows," said Faneca, who had clearly been won over by the rookie. "I mean, come on, just under two minutes, and he steps up, calls the plays, make the throws—that's *huge*."

The Steelers beat the New York Jets at Heinz Field, which upped their record to 12-1 and clinched the AFC North Division title for the eighth time in Cowher's 13 years with the team.

"It's the first step, and you have to enjoy it," said the coach. "This football team has been very focused, and they understand that we're still on a journey."

The win over the Chad Pennington-quarterbacked Jets coming on the heels of the win over Leftwich and the Jaguars, gave Roethlisberger back-to-back victories over the two former Marshall quarterbacks, although neither Pennington nor Roethlisberger had a particularly good game.

The day actually belonged to Bettis and Curtis Martin, the Jets' tailback, because they each pushed their career rushing totals past the 13,000-yard mark, a line that has been crossed only six times in NFL history. *The Bus* also threw a scoring pass, and scored the last touchdown, his 12th of the season, a single-season high for the 33-year-old.

"Age is a number, just like a shoe size," declared Bettis. "It doesn't mean anything. The only way to judge a player is by their ability, and I still have ability."

The Steelers traveled east the following week to play the Giants, and they had their hands full against a team that came into the contest with a 5-8 record. Eli Manning had been given the starting job a month earlier, but he had struggled in each of his four starts. The Giants' rookie put up decent numbers against Pittsburgh's top-ranked defense, however, and forced the Steelers to play catch-up throughout the game—despite Roethlisberger's first 300-yard passing day as a pro—until Bettis finally punched across a late-fourth-quarter touchdown that put Pittsburgh over the top, 33-30.

Roethlisberger was well on his way to delivering a win in the Steelers' next game after he threw a third-quarter touchdown pass that gave Pittsburgh a 17-7 lead over the Ravens, the only team to have blemished the Steelers' otherwise perfect record. On the play, however, Baltimore linebacker Terrell Suggs drove the quarterback into the ground right after he'd released the ball. The vicious and illegal hit sent Roethlisberger to the sidelines with an injury to his ribs, so Tommy Maddox came onto the field and finished up the Steelers' 20-7 victory.

Since they had already clinched the No. 1 seeding in the AFC, Cowher decided to keep Roethlisberger and his sore ribs out of Pittsburgh's final regular-season game against Buffalo, which the Steelers won, 29-24. The victory upped their record to 15-1 as they became only the fourth team in league history to win 15 games in the regular season.

Roethlisberger, who won a rookie-record 13 starts and broke Dan Marino's rookie records for passer rating and completion percentage, became the first quarterback ever to be named the Rookie of the Year by the Associated Press, which is a nationwide panel of football writers and broadcasters. *The Sporting News*, whose award is based upon voting by the league's pro scouting directors, also named him the Rookie of the Year.

"I think it's great," said Cowher, who was named the Coach of the Year by *The Sporting News*. "When you look at what he's done and the way he came in and handled everything, it was simply a no-brainer. It was a well- deserved validation."

Although Roethlisberger appreciated the recognition, his focus was on the Steelers' upcoming playoff game against the Jets, which he hoped would prove to be a springboard to a victory in the Super Bowl.

"It's an honor, but I consider it a team award, because I wouldn't have won it without my teammates," said the quarterback. "Everything that has happened this season has been so special, but awards aren't what this team is about. We've been striving for one goal since the start of the season, and we need to win three more games to attain that goal."

The Steelers took the first step toward their objective with a 20-17 overtime win over the Jets, although to do so they had to survive a pair of second-half interceptions thrown by Roethlisberger and a fourth-quarter fumble by Bettis, his first in 353 touches dating back to the previous season, as well as two late missed field goal attempts by the Jets' kicker.

"I know what I did wrong," said Roethlisberger, who had also thrown the fourth quarter touchdown pass that tied the game at 17-17 and then led the offense on the overtime drive that won the game. "I came in and watched the game on tape, just to get an understanding of the mistakes that I made. But I can't dwell any more on this game, because I need to shift my focus to the Patriots, and I can't play like a rookie against them, like I did against the Jets, or we'll definitely lose the game."

Unfortunately for Roethlisberger and the Steelers, he played poorly, again, and the Patriots won the AFC Championship Game, 41-27, and then went on to beat the

Eagles in the Super Bowl. And what made the loss and the missed opportunity even harder to accept was the fact that the Steelers had beaten both the Patriots and the Eagles earlier in the season.

"I feel like a let a lot of people down, but it was a good starting year for me," said Roethlisberger, who threw a pair of touchdown passes and a trio of interceptions. "We didn't go as far as we wanted to, but we had a good season, until this last game. Hopefully, it will serve as a building block for what we want to do in the future."

 BEN ROETHLISBERGER

7 SATISFACTION

In their tear-filled moments following the loss to the Patriots, Roethlisberger made an outlandish promise to Jerome Bettis, who had spoken about retiring from the game.

"He said if I came back, he'd win a Super Bowl for me," said Bettis, who had never even had the opportunity to win an AFC title, let alone hoist the Vince Lombardi Trophy, during his first 12 seasons in the league. "So, I decided to give it one more try."

Roethlisberger then proceeded to do everything that he could to deliver on that promise, beginning with his decision to start his preparations for the 2005 season only a few weeks after the loss to the Patriots.

"It was important for me because I didn't play as well as I could have or should have in the playoffs," he explained. "I wanted to get back into it and redeem myself so, hopefully, it doesn't happen again. I wanted to try to get better in all aspects of my game, both mentally and physically."

The second-year pro also felt more comfortable with his role on the team and with his teammates.

"Last year at this time I was just getting ready for the draft," he noted. "There were so many unanswered questions. Now I know what's going on. I'm working on offense, working on my body. This year is a lot more fun, a lot less stressful. The guys know me now, I know their names, and I can just enjoy being a Steeler. I'm not walking on eggshells anymore."

The one concern that Cowher had about Roethlisberger was that he might have unrealistic expectations for himself.

"I think the biggest thing for him is to not get caught up in the result of each game, but just to focus on the process," said the coach. "That's going to be very important for him. We're not going to have another 15-1 season, and we're not asking him to carry the team. We just want him to be a leader and, like everybody else, to be accountable, and to continue to grow."

The Steelers played like a team on a mission in their opening game, as they scored on their first six possessions and leveled the Tennessee Titans, 34-7. Roethlisberger did his part by throwing for two touchdowns and posting a perfect 158.3 passer rating, becoming the first quarterback since 2003 to attain a perfect rating.

Roethlisberger was nearly as effective the following week, as he connected with Hines Ward on two scoring passes, and led the Steelers to a 27-7 win over the Houston Texans. Willie Parker, who had taken on the role as the starting running back after injuries to Bettis and Duce Staley, also had a big day, as he ran for 161 yards, and helped carry the Steelers to their 16th consecutive regular-season win, which tied them for the second-best run in NFL history. By a coincidence of their schedule, Pittsburgh's next game was against the Patriots, the team whose 18-game winning streak they had brought to an end a year earlier.

The Steelers looked as though they might be able to extend their streak after Roethlisberger threw his second touchdown pass of the day to Ward, which brought them into a 20-20 tie with 1:21 left in regulation time. But that was all the time that Tom Brady needed to drive New England into Pittsburgh territory and position the ball for

Adam Vinatieri's game-winning field goal. The loss not only ended the Steelers' streak, it also snapped Roethlisberger's perfect 15-0 regular-season run.

The Steelers got right back on the horse, however, the following week in San Diego by beating the Chargers on a Monday night, 24-22, with a game-winning drive that was capped by Jeff Reed's field goal with only :06 left to play. Roethlisberger, who had been injured three plays prior to Reed's kick, was sidelined for their next game, a 23-17 loss in OT to Jacksonville. But he was back in the saddle the following week and threw for two touchdowns, as the Steelers beat the Bengals, 27-13. Pittsburgh's running backs also had a big day, as they galloped for 221 yards.

"This is what we do," said Bettis. "And until you stop us, we're going to keep doing it."

The Steelers won their second Monday night game of the season by repeating the same nail-biting formula they had used in the previous one, with Roethlisberger leading the team on another late-game drive that ended with Reed splitting the uprights to give them a 20-19 win over the Ravens.

The right-knee injury that Roethlisberger had suffered in the San Diego game worsened, and he was forced to undergo surgery, which sidelined him for the next three games.

With first Batch and then Maddox stepping in to replace Roethlisberger, the Steelers won two of the three games, which brought their record to 7-3 and put them in position to make a playoff run. But, despite the return of Roethlisberger, they lost their next two games—27-7 to the undefeated Colts and 38-31 to the Bengals—which dropped their record to 7-5 and put their playoff hopes in jeopardy.

"We know that our back is against the wall," said Duce

Staley. "But any time a wounded animal has his back against the wall, he either comes out fighting or he dies. This team is not going to die."

The Steelers reacted exactly as Staley had said they would, as they closed out their season with four straight wins, and secured a spot in the post-season tournament with an 11-5 mark. Unlike 2004, when they had topped the AFC's playoff seedings, this year they were at the very bottom, but Roethlisberger was feeling a lot better in his second go-round.

"I feel more comfortable going into the playoffs now," said the quarterback, who had thrown five interceptions in his two previous playoff games. "Last year, I was kind of, 'Oh my gosh, I'm so nervous, here we go, don't make a mistake.' I'm not going to go out and play scared this year. I'm going to go out and play as well as I can and try to help this team win."

The Steelers took their first step up the playoff ladder by beating the Bengals in Cincinnati, 31-17, as Roethlisberger threw for a trio of touchdown passes, and posted a near-perfect 148.7 quarterback rating.

"That's what an extra year of experience will do for a player," noted Cowher. "He's been there before, and he knows what it takes."

The Steelers traveled to Indianapolis for their next game, and arrived with a collective chip on their shoulders because almost no one gave them a chance against Peyton Manning and the Colts, who had compiled an NFL-best 14-2 record. But Pittsburgh took it right to the Colts, as Roethlisberger connected on a pair of first-quarter touchdown passes, and the Steelers hung on to topple the Colts, 21-18. In addition to his two scoring passes, Roethlisberger made the play of the day with 1:01 left on the clock, when he made a game-saving, open-field tackle that prevented Colts' cornerback Nick Harper from turning a Bettis fumble into a last minute touchdown.

"Once in a blue moon, Jerome fumbles, and, once in a blue moon, I make a tackle," said Roethlisberger, completely understating his spectacular play. "They just happened to occur in the same day."

"I can't tell you how much Ben's tackle meant to me," said Bettis. "I didn't want to cost my team a playoff win and have my career end with a fumble."

While Roethlisberger's tackle had propelled the Steelers forward into the AFC Championship game, some of their players couldn't resist taking one final look backwards.

"When I watched the sports shows this week, the analysts weren't even breaking down our game," noted linebacker Larry Foote. "They just said that Indianapolis was going to beat Pittsburgh—end of story. But once the whistle blows, all that stuff is out the window,"

The Steelers took their traveling road show to Denver and blew out the Broncos in the AFC title game, 34-17, as Roethlisberger continued his splendid post-season play by throwing for a pair of touchdowns and running for one, while completing 21 of 29 pass attempts and compiling a 124.9 quarterback rating.

"He just has this relentless quality about him," said Kendall Simmons, Pittsburgh's right guard. "He's a second-year guy, but he plays like he's been in the league 10 years. He sets the tone for our offense."

The Steelers had knocked off the three top seeds in the AFC during their stunning playoff run, and had earned the right to continue on their journey to Detroit to meet the

Seattle Seahawks in Super Bowl XL.

"We've been knocking on this door for years," said Pittsburgh cornerback Deshea Townsend, referring to the fact that the Steelers had lost their three most recent AFC Championship Games, including 1997, 2001 and 2004. "We decided that it was time to quit knocking, so we came here and kicked it down."

The Seahawks struck first when Josh Brown opened the scoring with a first-quarter field goal, but the Steelers vaulted into the lead in the second quarter when Roethlisberger dove into the end zone from a yard out. The team took that 7-3 lead into the locker room, while the halftime intermission was being provided by the Rolling Stones, who delighted the fans with a medley of their all-time hits, including *(I can't get no) Satisfaction*, which was ranked as No. 1 on VH1's list of the 100 greatest Rock & Roll songs.

On the second offensive play after the intermission, Willie Parker electrified the crowd at Ford Field by exploding for a 75-yard touchdown run, the longest rushing play in Super Bowl history. The Seahawks matched that touchdown later in the quarter, to close the gap to 14-10. And, that's the way the score stood until 8:56 of the fourth quarter, when the Steelers' pulled a trick play out of their bag and Randle El, who had been a college quarterback, took a direct snap from center and threw a strike to Hines Ward for a 43-yard touchdown that closed out the scoring in the Steelers' 21-10 Super Bowl triumph.

"We went to three different cities and shocked the world three different times, and then we came here and did it again," said linebacker Joey Porter. "We weren't supposed to be in this situation, but we pulled it off. We took the toughest scenic route and pulled it off everywhere we went."

Although Roethlisberger didn't have a particularly good game, he still rejoiced in the win that allowed the Steelers to climb the last rung on their post-season ladder and join the Dallas Cowboys and the San Francisco 49ers as the only franchises to have hoisted the Vince Lombardi Trophy five times.

"My teammates picked me up, the offensive line played great, the running game came around in the second half," said Roethlisberger, a big smile set across his face. "I can't thank them enough. If this is my only one, I'll take it."

Right after the game ended, Roethlisberger and Bettis shared a long bear hug, embracing each other and celebrating a promise kept.

"It's been an incredible ride, and I couldn't ask for anything better," said Bettis, who was able, at long last, to gain his *Satisfaction* and announce his retirement while he was surrounded by his family and teammates, and in the city where he was born. *"The Bus* has made his last stop."

8 ALWAYS A STEELER

Just four months after he had become the youngest quarterback in history to win a Super Bowl, Roethlisberger was sprawled on a Pittsburgh street, with multiple head and facial injuries, including a broken nose, a fractured jaw, and a concussion, which might have been avoided if he had been wearing a helmet.

In the blink of an eye, his life almost turned from triumph to tragedy on a beautiful June morning, when the motorcycle he was driving collided with an automobile and he was thrown into the windshield of the car.

His family and teammates gathered at the hospital that afternoon as he was prepped for surgery.

"I was with our dad at an AAU tournament in Cincinnati when we got the news," said his sister Carlee. "It was the longest car trip ever, because you think. 'What did I say or not say to him?' It was such a relief when we knew that his injuries weren't life-threatening and that he would be all right."

Coach Cowher had been among the people who had asked Roethlisberger to stop riding his motorcycle, a message that was ignored, even after Cleveland Browns' tight end Kellen Winslow Jr. had suffered a season-ending injury in a motorcycle crash the year before.

"I told him that he only has a small time in his life to play football, and that he should be careful about what he chooses to do," said Cowher. "He told me that he wouldn't stop driving, but added that he wasn't really a risk-taker and that he would drive carefully. I guess I didn't get through to him."

Eventually, however, Roethlisberger decided that the risks outweighed the rewards.

Although Roethlisberger escaped critical injuries, his recovery from the accident set back his preparation for the 2006 season, and it wasn't until the third of their four pre-season games that he finally started to feel mentally and physically ready for the challenge of helping the Steelers try to defend their Super Bowl title.

"When I first got here, I almost felt like a rookie all over again," said Roethlisberger. "But now it's starting to come back to me. I'm starting to feel comfortable, starting to get in the groove with my timing with the receivers and the offensive line, and I'm feeling mentally sharper. I'm starting to get in the flow, see the field, and make better decisions."

Five days before the start of the season, however, Roethlisberger was back in the hospital having an emergency appendectomy, which may have been a fallout from the crash.

After watching Pittsburgh win their opening game of the season, Roethlisberger was back in action the following week, but he was ineffective and the Steelers dropped a 9-0 game to the Jaguars.

"I wasn't making plays I need to make," admitted Roethlisberger, who threw two interceptions and had only 141 passing yards. "I have to apologize not only to our offense, but to our defense, too."

Despite his apologies, his performances continued to be sub-par over the course of the next two games, both of which went into the loss column. Four games into the season following their Super Bowl win, the Steelers were 1-3, and Roethlisberger had already thrown five interceptions, while failing to throw a single touchdown pass. But he snapped out of his funk the following week by throwing his first two touchdown passes of the 2006 season, and the Steelers crushed the Kansas City Chiefs, 45-7. He followed that with a strong effort against the Atlanta Falcons, although he was forced out of the game with a concussion, and the Steelers lost the game. They also lost their next two games, as Roethlisberger threw seven more interceptions, and they reached the halfway mark of the schedule with a 2-6 record.

It was time to stick a fork in the Steelers' season.

"It seemed like every time I got back on track, something else came to take its place," said Roethlisberger. "I finally just had to laugh at all of it and tell myself, 'That's just the way things are going this year.'"

Despite yet more uneven play by Roethlisberger, the Steelers did manage to turn their record upside down during the second half of 2006 by going 6-2 and finishing with an 8-8 record. For Roethlisberger, though, the end of the season couldn't have come soon enough.

"I actually felt fine once I got going in the season," said Roethlisberger, who threw 23 interceptions—three more than he had totaled in his first two seasons—while his completion percentage dropped to a career-low 59.7. "But once it was over, it was, like, I'm done; let's put it behind me and move on."

Bruce Arians, Pittsburgh's offensive coordinator even saw a good side to Roethlisberger's humbling struggles.

"Every quarterback needs one of those years," said Arians. "You don't win a Super Bowl every year, or win

13 in a row every year. A little dose of this reality can be helpful in the future, if you learn from the adversity. And, when you bounce back, you earn more respect than you had before."

A few weeks after the end of the 2006 season, Bill Cowher, who had been the team's head coach for 15 years, decided to step away from the constant grind and spend more time with his family.

"There comes a time in your life when you have to prioritize," explained Cowher, who had been in the NFL since 1979, when he entered the league as a free-agent linebacker with the Eagles. "My family has made a lot of sacrifices for me, and now I'm looking forward to being there for them."

After the Steelers' front office had interviewed a number of candidates, they decided to replace Cowher with Mike Tomlin, who had been in the league as an assistant coach for six seasons, most recently as the defensive coordinator for the Minnesota Vikings.

The Tomlin regime got off to a high-flying start when Pittsburgh opened the 2007 season by battering the Browns, 34-7, and Roethlisberger put on a passing clinic by throwing four touchdown passes, one more than his previous single-game best. They won their next game in convincing style, too, as they beat the Bills, 26-3, to earn the 500th win in franchise history. The Steelers quickly took their first step toward the next new milestone the following week, when they out-classed the 49ers, 37-17, and ran their record to 3-0.

The Steelers were pumped after opening their season with three impressive wins. They had outscored their opponents 97-26, and Willie Parker had rushed for more than 100-yards in each of the games, while Big Ben, with six touchdown passes and only one interception, was leading the offense and playing with a high level of skill.

But they hit a bump in the road the following week in Arizona, when the Cardinals picked off two of Roethlisberger's passes, including one in the shadow of their own goal line, and came away with a 21-14 win.

"This loss is on me," said Roethlisberger, as he explained the pick he had thrown from the Cardinals' 4-yard line. "When I let the pass go, I thought it was a touchdown. I didn't see their safety."

The Steelers seemed to get back in step the following week, when they whitewashed the Seahawks, 21-0, but then they stumbled off the path and were beaten by the Broncos, 31-28. Once again, Roethlisberger played the role of Santa Claus, as he turned the ball over to Denver on two first-half picks and also coughed up a fumble that was returned for a touchdown.

He did his best to make up for those miscues by playing a brilliant second half and rallying the Steelers to a 28-28 tie, but he couldn't quite get them out in front of the eight-ball he had put them behind.

"It was disappointing because the first half was on us, it really wasn't what they did," said Roethlisberger, who passed for four touchdowns, including three after the half-time break. "But we made some huge plays in the second half, and we can build on that."

The Steelers, did in fact, seem to use the Denver game as a foundation for success, because they went on to win their next three games, with Roethlisberger playing the part of the master builder. They started the streak with a routine 24-13 victory in Cincinnati, which was keyed by a pair of touchdown passes from Roethlisberger to Hines Ward. But there was nothing ordinary about the 38-7 beating they administered to Baltimore, as Big Ben established a career high with five touchdown passes, all in the first half.

Steelers' linebacker James Harrison, who had sacked Roethlisberger four times in Harrison's final game at Kent State, had 3.5 sacks against the Ravens to go along with three forced fumbles, an interception and a fumble recovery.

"Those two guys were spectacular," said Mike Tomlin. "They put on quite a show."

Although the scenario changed the following week the result was just as stunning, as Roethlisberger rallied the Steelers with two second-half touchdown passes and a 30-yard scoring run to lead Pittsburgh past Cleveland, 31-28.

"I've been in this league seven, eight years now and this is the first time I've been around a quarterback like him," Tomlin said. "I've been around elite guys at other positions, but the reality is when you have an elite quarterback you always have the chance to win. Ben gives us that opportunity."

But the Steelers' high-powered offense suddenly stalled over the next two games, a 19-16 loss to the 1-8 Jets, and a 3-0 win against a Dolphins team that finished the season at 1-15.

Pittsburgh managed to put a charge back in their battery the following week with a 24-10 win over the Bengals, as Roethlisberger ran for one score and threw a pair of TD passes to Hines Ward. The second touchdown reception by Ward was the 64th of his Steelers' career, breaking the record of 63 that had been held by former Pittsburgh standout, John Stallworth.

"I'm incredibly proud and honored to be the one who

threw the ball to him, and to have the opportunity to play with someone like Hines," said Roethlisberger.

The win, which upped the Steelers record to 9-3, seemed to mark them as one of the top teams in the league, but then they shed some luster by losing three of their final four games to finish the regular season with a 10-6 record.

"We're not playing well enough to win right now," said Tomlin. "That's the cold reality of it. The answers to our problems are in our locker room."

Although the Steelers had limped to the finish line, they had still made it into the playoff picture, and had an opportunity to provide the answers that Tomlin had been looking for by beating the Jaguars in a wild-card game. But Roethlisberger helped put the Steelers in a 21-7 first-half hole by having three of his passes picked off. Then, as if a switch had been turned from off to on, he led a furious second-half rally that propelled Pittsburgh into a 29-28 lead with 6:21 left to play. The Jaguars retook the lead, 31-29, on a Josh Scobee field goal with :37 left, and the Steelers had, finally, run out of answers.

"We staged a great comeback and showed a lot of heart, but a loss is a loss," said Roethlisberger. "It hurts."

Despite that disappointing end to the season, Roethlisberger, who established career highs in touchdown passes and quarterback rating, raised his game to a higher level in 2007 and created hope for even greater triumphs in the future.

Steelers management confirmed their commitment to Roethlisberger during the off-season by signing him to one of the richest contracts in league history.

"He is a Steeler, and he will always be a Steeler," said team owner Dan Rooney. "We are very pleased about that, and what it means for our future."

"This is a great birthday present to know that I'm going to be in Pittsburgh for a long time," said Roethlisberger, who signed the contract the day after his actual birth date. "I told them that I didn't want to go anywhere else the first day that I walked in here in 2004. We have a great organization and I love Pittsburgh and our fans. I don't want to go anywhere. I'm just growing as a leader, and as a quarterback, and I believe that we have all the pieces to the puzzle for the 2008 season. I think we have the makings of a championship football team."

Kevin Colbert, the director of football operations for the Steelers, knows that whatever other building blocks the Steelers might need to win another title, he already has the keystone.

"To me, a franchise is only as good as your quarterback," said Colbert "Fortunately, we have a great one."

ORDER FORM

QTY

TONY ROMO * BEN ROETHLISBERGER: A dual-biography of two football superstars. The book includes 16 pages of action-packed color photographs. 144 pages, 5 x 8. $5.99 US.   ____

TOM BRADY * LADAINIAN TOMLINSON: A dual-biography of two of the NFL's top players. The book includes 16 action-packed color photos. 144 pages, 5 x 8. $5.99 US.   ____

SUPERSTAR QUARTERBACKS: Includes biographical sketches and 18 full-color photos of six top quarterbacks: Peyton Manning, Eli Manning, Vince Young, Philip Rivers, Tony Romo and Drew Brees. 32 pages, 6 x 9. $3.99 US.   ____

BRETT FAVRE: An easy-to-read photo-filled biography of one of football's all-time greats. Written especially for younger children. 32 pages, 8 x 8. $4.50 US.   ____

BASEBALL SUPERSTARS ALBUM 2007: Includes 16 full-sized, full-color photos of 16 of the game's top players—including Derek Jeter, Albert Pujols, Ryan Howard, and Justin Morneau—plus biographical sketches and career stats. 48 pages, 8-1/2 x 11. $6.99 US.   ____

EXTREME ACTION STARS: Includes 15 action-packed photos and biographical sketches of Shaun White, Danny Way, Travis Pastrana, Bucky Lasek, and Blair Morgan. 32 pages, 8-1/2 x 11. $4.99 US.   ____

SPECIAL OFFER: The books listed below are being offered for $1.00 each, plus normal shipping charges.

MARK McGWIRE: An easy-to-read photo-filled biography of one of baseball's all-time greats. 32 pages, 8 x 8. Originally published at $4.50 US.   ____

FOOTBALL'S SUPERSTAR ALBUM 2000: Includes 16 full-sized, full-color photos of 16 of the game's top players, plus biographical sketches and career stats. 48 pages, 8-1/2 x 11. Originally published at $4.99 US.   ____

Total number of Book(s) Ordered   ____

Add $1.50 per book if you want book(s) autographed by author.   ____

Total Cost of Books   ____

TAX (NY State residents must add appropriate sales tax)   ____

Shipping Charges (in the US) $2.25 per book, up to a maximum of $11.25 on orders of 10 or fewer books.   ____

TOTAL PAYMENT ENCLOSED: (All payments must be in US currency; checks and money orders only; credit cards not accepted).   ____

(Please print clearly.)

NAME _____

ADDRESS _____

CITY_____ STATE _____ ZIP CODE_____

SEND PAYMENTS TO: **EAST END PUBLISHING, LTD.**
                   18 Harbor Beach Road, Miller Pl., NY 11764

Discounts are available on orders of 25 or more books.
For details write or email: rjbrenner1@gmail.com

Terms are subject to change without notice.